Lawhorne suggests that the Court has integrated the First and Fourteenth amendments as follows: "Congress shall make no law . . . abridging freedom of speech, or of the press. . . . nor shall any State deprive any person of life, liberty, or property, without due process of law."

He further shows the step-by-step process that resulted in a constitutional privilege for discussion of all individuals involved in public issues, provided there was no knowing or reckless falsehood. He demonstrates the way in which the "public issue" standard was jettisoned to be replaced by a secondary constitutional privilege that allowed discussion containing defamatory falsehoods about private individuals, provided those falsehoods were not published negligently. Finally, he examines decisions of the Burger Court that have narrowly interpreted the judicially determined constitutional privileges, giving plaintiffs the benefit of doubt in their efforts to obtain damages for libelous falsehoods.

Drawing upon his more than twenty-five years as a journalism practitioner and educator, Clifton O. Lawhorne provides a highly useful exposition of the evolving nature of libel law in the United States.

Clifton O. Lawhorne is Professor of Journalism, University of Arkansas at Little Rock and served as Head of the Law Division of the Association for Education in Journalism during 1978–1979. His journalism career has followed the classic pattern from printer's apprentice to editor, with his most recent position having been editor of *Grassroots Editor*, the bimonthly journal for newspapermen.

HOWARD RUSK LONG, general editor of the New Horizons in Journalism series, is Director Emeritus of the School of Journalism, Southern Illinois University at Carbondale.

NEW HORIZONS IN JOURNALISM
Howard Rusk Long, *General Editor*

CLIFTON O. LAWHORNE

THE SUPREME
COURT
and Libel

Foreword by HOWARD RUSK LONG

SOUTHERN ILLINOIS UNIVERSITY PRESS
Carbondale and Edwardsville

Printed in the United States of America

Designed by *Design for Publishing*

Library of Congress Cataloging in Publication Data

Lawhorne, Clifton O
  The Supreme Court and libel.

  (New horizons in journalism)
  Includes index.
    1. Libel and slander—United States—Cases.
  2. United States. Supreme Court. I. Title.
  KF1266.A7L38   346.7303'4   80-21161
  ISBN 0-8093-0998-X

To HOWARD RUSK LONG

CONTENTS

FOREWORD

Until one encounters an analysis of the decision-making process within the membership of the Supreme Court of the United States one is inclined to assume that the principles of freedom and responsibility are as compatible as yin and yang. Was not much of the struggle of the American colonists against oppressions of royal and proprietory masters directed against the Star Chamber common law of sedition? Was not that issue settled when the states and commonwealths adopted the Constitution amended, in compromise, to guarantee freedom of religion, freedom of speech, freedom of the press, freedom of assembly, and the right to petition redress of grievances? Yes and no. Imperfect man, forever destined to create imperfect institutions, yet seeking to resolve the dilemma of his distaste of the monolithic and his fear of anarchy, by compromise, arrived at a compact intended to establish a rule of law to be sustained in debate and further compromise by the will of the governed in what we have learned to call democratic procedures.

One of the greatest imperfections inherent in the Constitution, a vaguely defined division of responsibilities between central government and its component parts, immediately spawned dissentions still unresolved in the dialectics of national sovereignty and states' rights. Strict constructionism prevailed until it was necessary by force of arms to prove once and for all that the whole is greater than the sum of the parts. As with the ten amendments called the Bill of Rights, again the Constitution was saved by synthesis achieved in the three revisions now known as the Reconstruction amendments. Within this framework of orderly procedure the democratic process today continues, with relatively minor and temporary instances of violence, in the form of ongoing popular debate with consensus

achieved at the ballot box. Dependent as they are upon the appro-
bation of the voters, elected officials of the executive and legislative
branches have always been responsive (as accurately as it could be
interpreted) to popular sentiment. Nor has the federal judiciary
been far behind. What began as a drift toward centralization, moti-
vated by expansionism on land and sea and the policy of internal
improvements in our time, under pressures of complex social and
economic problems—worldwide as well as internal—is seen as the
march of supergovernment.

Men and women still at work in editorial offices can recall the
standard procedures designed to guard against confrontation in
court under the rules of common-law defamation as modified from
state to state by statute. The man with the green eyeshade labored
under such contradictions as truth is a defense in this state and not
at all or only with limitations in the next. The word alleged (not
exactly without value today) was the magic stone of the police
reporter struggling to keep his job. Any journalist from that background can view only with benign understanding the confusion
among the justices of the Supreme Court as they attempted, in
response to pressures engendered by New Deal reform, to bring
order out of chaos in the realm of defamation law. The instances of
split decisions, plurality decisions, modification if not reversal of
their own decisions, individual self-contradiction together reflect
not ineptitude but the complexity of the problem and the difficulties
of achieving consensus in a fairly new arena. Moreover it is hearten-
ing to observe how the constitutional system of compromise retains
the relative effectiveness expected of it even in the most rarefied
forum of our governmental system.

Nothing reflects the sincerity of purpose motivating the contenti-
ousness of the individual justices more than the thread of consistency binding together the half century of decisions examined by
Professor Lawhorne than the universal concern of the jurists for
sustaining free and uninhibited discussion of all public issues. The
future, as Professor Lawhorne emphasizes, will bring additional
change. It may be safe to speculate shifts from left to right or right to
left with the moods of the electorate. Yet it will remain a fact that
the work of the Supreme Court of the United States at last has built
the foundation, or even more, for a body of constitutional law to
replace the disorderly mishmash of common and statutory law of

the various states. The concern of special interests aside, freedom of debate in the marketplace of ideas seems more secure than ever before in American history. It is comforting to observe that these rulings of the Court sustain an opinion oft expressed by this observer in the curbstone dictum: There is no footnote to the First Amendment that would disqualify either the ignoramous or the damned fool

Carbondale, Illinois   HOWARD RUSK LONG
4 July 1980

PREFACE

The fewer and fewer restrictions that have evolved in the jurisprudence of libel in the United States have closely reflected the growth of what the First Amendment to the Constitution calls "freedom of speech, or of the press." Further, the constriction of libel and the resulting expansion in freedom of discussion can be traced, to a large extent, through the decisions of the Supreme Court of the United States. And it is the purpose of this book to do just that. Emphasis is placed on the last fifty years—on the decisions of the Court since 1931, when libel laws of the states first began to be curtailed by new interpretations of the Constitution. To provide perspective, however, a cursory treatment is given to the adoption of the First Amendment, the early formulation of the law of libel, and a number of old but important decisions of the Court.

While the book takes a chronological approach, in the interest of clarity, it nevertheless focuses on the law of libel as it is today. Seven of the nine chapters deal with the rapid-fire Supreme Court decisions that have radically changed the law of libel in the United States over the past fifteen years. The treatment is thorough, but brief, and explanation is punctuated in a number of instances with key passages from the actual Court decisions. The effort has been to place these decisions in a meaningful context, to provide a ready handbook for communicators, educators, and perhaps even lawyers.

The reader is cautioned, however, that the current status of the law is not and cannot be final. The law is not static. It changes, sometimes slowly and sometimes rather rapidly. As Justice Oliver Wendell Holmes, Jr., observed in 1881, the law constantly adopts new principles from the experiences of life, from what is believed to be public policy at a given time, or from what is in a given instance understood to be convenient.[1] This, perhaps, is a major lesson of this book.

In chronicling the changes in the law of libel, this volume is divided into nine chapters. Chapter one deals with the early development of libel in the United States under Supreme Court interpretations that the First Amendment prevented only the national government—not the states—from interfering with press freedom. Chapter two shows a shift in interpretations that resulted, after World War I, in the Supreme Court's declaring a state's prior restraint on libel as unconstitutional and, after World War II, in the Supreme Court's asserting a power to nullify state libel decisions that encroached on press freedom. This chapter details how the Court tied the First and Fourteenth amendments together, somewhat in the following "shorthand" fashion: "Congress shall make no law . . . abridging freedom of speech, or of the press. . . . nor shall any State deprive any person of life, liberty, or property, without due process of law." The remaining chapters show how the Court's actions used these constitutional amendments to systematically nullify state laws.

Specifically, chapter three tells how in 1964 the Warren Court formulated a nationwide privilege to falsely libel public officials, in their official conduct, provided publications were not made with knowledge of falsity or reckless disregard of falsity. Chapter four details how this privilege was reinterpreted to include even libels about officials' private behavior that affected official conduct, to include criminal as well as civil libel, and to encompass discussion of government employees thought to have substantial responsibility for controlling government issues. Chapter five examines the still further expansion of this privilege of discussion, short of the knowing or reckless falsehood, to public figures. And chapter six recounts a series of cases involving editorials, candidates, accusations of crime, television broadcasts, city council meetings and government reports—all of which more clearly defined and explained the constitutional privilege to discuss public figures and public officials.

Chapter seven discusses an opinion by a deeply divided Court, after a shift in chief justices, that resulted in a short-lived constitutional privilege for discussion of all individuals involved in public issues—provided there was no knowing or reckless falsehood.

Chapter eight details how the "public-issue" standard was jettisoned and replaced with a secondary constitutional privilege allowing discussion with defamatory falsehoods about private individuals, provided those falsehoods were not published negligently. Finally, chapter nine examines decisions of the Burger Court that have narrowly interpreted the judicially determined constitutional privileges, giving plaintiffs the benefit of doubt in their efforts to obtain damages for libelous falsehoods.

Despite the fluctuation in the Court's philosophy from time to time—including the subtle shift by today's Court—the decisions show a continuous march for freedom of speech and press. They do not, by any means, show the extremely broad picture relating to free speech and press. But they do show a meaningful picture in an important area. It is this picture, concerning libel alone, that is presented to the reader.

In writing this book, I have drawn on understandings gained from classrooms and colleagues and from some twenty-five years experience as a journalism practitioner and educator. Hopefully these understandings and experiences have provided adequate background for proper interpretations of the law. I do not, however, expect an error-free presentation and am quick to admit that the errors are mine alone. Nevertheless I was not alone in this project and would like to gratefully acknowledge the support given by Dr. Leonard A. Granato and Mrs. Nell Rorie of the University of Arkansas at Little Rock. Additionally I am particularly thankful for the expert assistance of my wife, Claudetta, and the most excellent work of Teresa White, who as an editor of the Southern Illinois University Press has been my "backstop" for two books. Above all, though, I wish to single out Dr. Howard R. Long, my mentor since graduate studies at Southern Illinois University. His suggestions, advice, and guidance have been invaluable. To him, I dedicate this book.

Little Rock, Arkansas   CLIFTON O. LAWHORNE
July 1980

PROLOGUE

With the settlement of the American colonies, English rulers brought with them the common law of libel as it had evolved from early Star Chamber decisions in that country. Under this English common law, a libel was defined as a publication that "robs a man of his good name, which ought to be more precious to him than his life."[1] The publishers and disseminators of libels were held strictly accountable, ostensibly to prevent breeches of the peace and scandal of government. This, too, was a Star Chamber philosophy, which had been officially formulated in the 1606 *Case de Libellis Famosis,* as follows:

> Every libel . . . is made either against a private man, or against a magistrate or public person. If it be against a private man it deserves a severe punishment, for although the libel be made against one, yet it incites all those of the same family, kindred, or society to revenge, and so tends . . . to quarrels and breach of the peace, and may be the cause of shedding of blood, and of great inconvenience: if it be against a magistrate, or other public person, it is a greater offense, for it concerns not only a breach of the peace, but also the scandal of Government; for what greater scandal of Government can there be than to have corrupt or wicked magistrates to be appointed and constituted by the King to govern his subjects under him? And greater imputation to the State cannot be, than to suffer such corrupt men to sit in the sacred seat of justice, or to have any meddling in or concerning the administration of justice.[2]

The Star Chamber in this case also set the English precedent that was to last in that country until 1843—that it made no difference whether the libel was true or false.[3] To publish any "ill opinions" whatsoever of either public or private individuals—by writing, verse, pictures, or signs—was punishable as a crime. Further, judges, not juries, determined whether publications were libelous and then set the punishment—often death.[4] Juries had but one task—to determine the "fact" that the accused did or did not publish or disseminate the libel.

This law was followed exactly in the first recorded colonial prosecution, that of church elder Roger Williams, who was banished from the Massachusetts Bay Colony after circulating "letters of defamation" accusing the General Court there of oppression in religion.[5] From that point on, however, the English common law of libel was severely bent in the American colonies.

A change came with the first libel trial of a printer, William Bradford, in 1692. Here Quaker judges in Philadelphia did not follow the English practice of determining libel. Instead, they allowed a jury to make this determination, and Bradford was acquitted because of indecision.[6] Furthermore, his codefendant, Peter Boss, was allowed to introduce evidence of the truth as justification for the libel charged against him.[7] Four years later in Massachusetts, the author Thomas Maule, in his plea to the jury, claimed he wrote only spiritual truths in a Quaker book, and the jury refused to declare his claimed truths a libel.[8] Then, in 1698 in Virginia, Gerald Slye was sentenced only after he could not prove the truth of letters he wrote criticizing Gov. Francis Nicholson.[9] Another critic of Nicholson, Philip Clark, was found guilty on the basis of spreading news that was false.[10] The question of libel again was turned over to jurors in 1723, in Massachusetts, when John Checkley was tried for publishing a religious pamphlet. The jury came in with the following verdict: "If the book is false and scandalous libel, we find him guilty. . . . But if the said Book, containing a discourse concerning Episcopacy, be not a false and scandalous libel; then we find him not guilty."[11] These were all cases involving libel of government, and criminal cases. Yet jurors were determining fact and law in some cases, and truth was a factor.

Still it was not until the 1735 trial of the publisher John Peter Zenger that the defense of truth and jury determination of libel were joined as primary points of consideration in the public's mind. This was a newspaper case, and it received considerable publicity, both in the colonies and in England, where it was reported in *How-*

ell's State Trials.[12] Zenger, publisher of the *New-York Weekly Journal,* was tried for printing criticism of Gov. William Cosby. At his trial, a runaway jury took both determination of the law and fact despite the judge's instructions.[13] And while jurors found Zenger published the criticism, that criticism was found to be true and hence not libelous.[14]

This was considered by many historians as a turning point in the law. While not recognized as law in England or by crown representatives in the colonies, it had tremendous popular support.[15] And the precedent did have effect. Six years later, Thomas Fleet, publisher of the *Boston Evening Post,* thwarted a libel prosecution by producing five witnesses to prove the truth of a story critical of Sir Robert Walpole, the British prime minister.[16] And the earliest history of printing in this country tells the story of William Parks, publisher of the *Williamsburg Gazette* in Virginia, who was exonerated of a libel charge in the 1740s by proving the truth of a "sheep-stealing" charge he made against a member of the Virginia House of Burgess.[17]

There are, however, numerous instances in which colonial legislatures punished publishers for libelous utterances that were officially called "breaches of privilege" or "contempt of legislature."[18] And here truth or falsity was not considered. This, though, was a different arena. The libel cases in the courts themselves were unique. Two threads of consistency held these trials together. One was justification of libel by truth; the other was jury determination as to whether libel was actually involved.

And this thread was carried through to the heightened period of discontent between 1766 and the Revolution, when authorities found it almost impossible to obtain libel indictments.[19] As an example, when the Massachusetts Council ordered Isaiah Thomas, publisher of the *Massachusetts Spy,* indicted in 1771 for criticizing Gov. Thomas Hutchinson, Thomas republished the Zenger doctrine that truth justified a libel. The result was refusal by the grand jury to bring in an indictment.[20]

Similarly when Alexander McDougall was jailed in an aborted prosecution for libeling the New York Assembly in the same year, the Zengerian principles were revived. In fact, a sort of propaganda warfare broke out in the New York press concerning truth as a defense in libel suits. The *New York Gazette and Post Boy* and the

New York Journal said it was. They said the Zenger principles were the public policy of the colonies in libel suits. The *Journal* even issued a fifty-three-page pamphlet containing the entire Zenger trial report.[21] This was countered by still another newspaper, also named the *New York Gazette,* published by Hugh Gaine, termed by journalism histories as a "turncoat" in the War for Independence. Gaine's *Gazette* published a sixty-page pamphlet in support of the English common law of libel, stating juries determined only the fact of publication while judges determined libel and punishment, without consideration of truth or falsity.[22]

Those who published newspapers, then, disagreed as to the law of libel. In a sense, they reflected the divided views of the colonists, who were on the threshold of discarding their English ties. The issue was not determined in the McDougall case, as the death of the only witness canceled the libel trial. Obviously, though, many advanced a law different from that in England. The popular concept—and a very real colonial heritage—was that juries determined libel on the basis of truth or falsity.[23]

This, though, is prologue. It came before the Declaration of Independence. Nevertheless, it set the stage for the development of the law of libel in a new nation.

THE SUPREME
COURT
and Libel

1/ Early Views of the Constitution
States Not Bound by Free Press Guarantee

When state conventions ratified the Constitution of the United States, the price exacted of Congress was a Bill of Rights for all citizens.[1] Such a bill was hammered out by Congress in its first session, and the result was the first Ten Amendments to the Constitution, which went into effect 15 December 1791. This Bill of Rights was led, then as now, by an amendment central to the individual's freedom to think, believe, associate, and communicate. Specifically, the First Amendment stated: "Congress shall make no law respecting an establishment of religion, or prohibiting the free exercise thereof; or abridging the freedom of speech, or of the press; or the right of the people peaceably to assemble, and to petition the Government for a redress of grievances."[2] The words were quite clear. Obviously, however, there was no uniform clarity, then as now, as to what "freedom of speech, or of the press" actually meant. Further, it quickly became evident that members of Congress felt that a free press was responsible for what was published and that a law could be passed to punish libels. Within seven years after the First Amendment stated "no law" could be passed restricting press freedom, Congress adopted the Sedition Law of 1798, which made it a crime to libel the government, the president, or Congress.

The law was passed at a time when many felt that there should be no libel against government, that United States independence had killed the old English common law of seditious libel that had been enforced in the colonies.[3] And there was basis for the belief. The few attempts in the states to prosecute for the crime of libel had been dropped by authorities or soundly rejected by juries.[4] And some of the early state constitutions had stipulated that citizens were free to investigate public officials in their public capacities and to truthfully report the results.[5] Further, it was felt that any federal libel action had been prohibited by a circuit court ruling that the national government could not prosecute for common-law crimes.[6]

Still, the Federalist members of Congress, then in power with the administration of Pres. John Adams, felt that elements of the opposition Republican press were making abusive and excessive attacks against the government as it prepared for an expected war with France.[7] Hence they passed the Sedition Law to muzzle this press criticism. The law, which went into effect on 14 July 1798 stated:

> If any person shall write, print, utter or publish . . . any false, scandalous and malicious writing or writings against the government of the United States, or . . . Congress . . . or the President . . . with intent to defame the said government or either house of . . . Congress, or the said President, or to bring them . . . into contempt or disrepute, or to excite against them . . . the hatred of the good people of the United States, or to stir up sedition within the United States . . . then such person, being thereof convicted . . . shall be punished by a fine not exceeding two thousand dollars, and by imprisonment not exceeding two years.[8]

Importantly, the law also stipulated that during trials those prosecuted could present the truth of the publications as a defense and that jurors could determine whether publications were libelous and publishers were guilty.

This last segment of the Sedition Law nationalized and formalized the right that had been asserted in the famed colonial libel trial of John Peter Zenger—the right to present truth in evidence and to have the jury make the determination as to libel.[9] Despite this, however, the law restricted actual press publication when no previous restrictions existed. Prior to the law, it had not been a federal crime to libel the government or its officers. With the law, it was. The Sedition Law had adopted the old English common-law concept that it was a crime to publish ill opinions of the government and public officials.

The prosecutions for this crime of criticism stirred up animosity and agitation all over the nation and was credited by some with toppling John Adam's presidency along with the Federalist party.[10] Questions as to the constitutionality of the law were widespread. For instance, it was called "expressly and positively" unconstitutional by the Virginia and Kentucky resolutions.[11] Despite the furor, though, judges consistently instructed jurors to ignore claims of unconstitutionality that were made by those prosecuted. Further, it was questionable as to whether two U.S. Supreme Court justices, William Patterson and Samuel Chase, afforded those they tried the moral, and perhaps legal, right to prove the truth of their statements. Presiding over circuit court trials, neither would allow witnesses to "link up" various portions of the truth. Each required all-inclusive truth from each witness, or no proof at all.[12] Chase's conduct in this respect, in the trial of James Callender, was a major cause for his later impeachment trial in Congress, though two-thirds vote was not attained in this only attempt to remove a Supreme Court justice.[13] Despite the highly publicized state trials by individual Supreme Court justices, however, the Court itself never had occasion to consider the constitutionality of the Sedition Law, which expired in less than three years, on 3 March 1801.[14]

Within this short period of time the Sedition Law had a tremendous effect on the jurisprudence of libel in this country. For one thing, it triggered a number of state common-law prosecutions for seditious libel, along with civil libel suits, and state authority to prosecute newspapers for attacks on government officials was firmly established.[15] For another, the law promoted the idea that truth was a defense to a charge of libeling government or its officials. This concept was quickly and broadly adopted in state laws, constitutions and courts.[16] All of this lends credence to a claim of one scholar living during the period that in the United States the "law of libel may be considered as commencing with the passing of the Sedition Law."[17]

This revived law of libel, however, was to become primarily a state matter. This was determined by the United States Supreme Court decision in the case of *United States* v. *Hudson and Goodwin* in 1812. This case was brought about because two Federalist editors, Barzillai Hudson and George Goodwin of the *Connecticut Courant,* published an article on 7 May 1806 attacking the then Republican party government, led by Pres. Thomas Jefferson. They charged Jefferson with bribing Napoleon Bonaparte to make a treaty with Spain for Florida and further claimed that Congress had secretely voted $2 million for the purpose. This publication caused a Republican U.S. attorney in Connecticut to secure a common-law indictment against the editors for seditious libel. However, circuit court judges differed on the constitutionality of a common-law libel prosecution in federal court. Hence the case was certified to the Supreme Court.

The Supreme Court finally handed down a decision in the case some six years after the indictment. The Court, in an opinion written by Justice William Johnson, said the only issue was whether United States courts had common-law jurisdiction in criminal cases. It said the answer had long since been settled in public opinion and that such jurisdiction had not been asserted for many years. Neither implied powers nor the Constitution gave "exercise of criminal jurisdiction in common law cases," the opinion stated.[18] Specifically, the opinion said the United States "possesses no jurisdiction but what is given them by the power that creates them."[19]

This decision, the Supreme Court's first in a libel case, effectively removed the United States courts from common-law prosecutions. So far as the federal courts were concerned, there no longer was a crime of libel. The only avenue left for common-law prosecutions was that of the state courts. And in state courts, criminal libel actions were rapidly being replaced with civil libel suits in which damages were awarded.[20]

States, then, became the arenas in which the laws of libel developed, and the development was not uniform. Both procedural and substantive differences evolved. Also while truth became, generally, a justification for defamatory falsehoods, states often required that truth be coupled with good motives and that publications be for justifiable ends.[21] Regardless of an individual state's specific rulings, however, those rulings were final and were not subject to review. This became quite clear in 1833, when the United States Supreme Court issued its opinion in the case of *Barron* v. *Mayor of Baltimore*.

This case resulted when John Barron sued the city of Baltimore for diverting a stream from his wharves, making them useless. He complained that the city had violated the Fifth Amendment to the U.S. Constitution, which states "private property shall not be taken for public use without just compensation."[22] But the Supreme Court held that the Fifth Amendment, and hence the entire Bill of Rights, "is intended solely as a limitation on the exercise of power by the government of the United States, and is not applicable to the legislation of the States."[23]

Citizens, then, were not protected from state infringements of rights stipulated in the first Ten Amendments. This meant, among other things, that libel decisions of the states could not be appealed to the United States Supreme Court on the grounds that First Amendment liberties had been abridged. Separate governmental spheres of sovereignty were firmly recognized by the decision.

Nevertheless, by constitutional mandate, the United States Supreme Court still retained some civil jurisdiction in libel cases. This included cases between citizens of different states, cases involving ambassadors and public ministers, and cases arising out of the Constitution and laws of the United States.[24] One such libel case, *White v. Nicholls,* arose in 1845. It involved a letter to the president from a group of Georgetown residents protesting political activities of the Georgetown collector of customs, Robert White, who had been appointed under a law of Congress.

While this pre–Civil War case did not involve the press, it was extremely important to the press. It was so because those who wrote the letter claimed it was not libelous because it was a "privileged communication." The Supreme Court, in an opinion written by Justice Peter V. Daniel, immediately recognized that the defense claims reached "much farther and to results infinitely higher" than the particular case. As the Court said:

> It involves this issue, so important to society, viz.: How far, under an alleged right to examine into the fitness and qualifications of men who are either in office or are applicants for office—or how far, under the obligation of a supposed duty to arraign such men either at the bar of their immediate superior, or that of public opinion, their reputation, their acts, their motives or feelings may be assailed with impunity—how far that law, designed for the protection of all, has placed a certain class of citizens without the pale of its protection?[25]

The overriding issue clearly was the extent to which privileged communications restricted public officials from securing libel judgments. Because of this, which the Court said related to the rights of individuals and to the good order of society, an extensive review of the common law of libel—civil libel—was undertaken.

From this review, the Court drew the following conclusions, "which we propound as the law applicable thereto:"

1. That every publication, either by writing, printing, or pictures, which charges upon or imputes to any person that which renders him liable to punishment, or which is calculated to make him infamous, or odious, or ridiculous, is *prima facie* a libel, and implies malice in the author and publisher towards the person concerning whom such publication is made. Proof of malice, therefore, in the cases just described, can never be required of the party complaining beyond the proof of the publication itself: justification, excuse, or extenuation, if either can be shown, must proceed from the defendant.

2. That the description of cases recognized as privileged communications must be understood as exceptions to this rule, and as being founded upon some apparently recognized obligation or motive, legal, moral, or social, which may fairly be presumed to have led to the publication and therefore *prima facie* relieves it from that just implication from which the general rule of law is deduced. The rule of evidence, as to such cases, is accordingly so far changed as to impose it on the plaintiff to remove those presumptions flowing from the seeming obligations and situations of the parties, and to require of him to bring home to the defendant the existence of malice as the true motive of his conduct.[26]

Basically the Court said that in regular libel cases, the burden was on the person sued to justify or excuse the publication. But in privileged communications, the burden of proof shifted. There could be no presumption of malice, and writers of privileged communications could not be held accountable unless express malice could be proved to the satisfaction of jurors.[27] Importantly, the Court went on to say that express malice could be shown if the complainant proved "falsehood and the absence of probable cause."[28]

Under the decision, then, those filing civil libel actions in cases involving privileged communications not only had to prove communications false but also had to prove that probable cause for the statements did not exist. Privilege here was assumed for a petition to a government official in a position to give redress for grievances. But the Court in this case also projected the view that privileged communications included reports in and of legislative or parliamentary proceedings, reports in and of judicial or legal proceedings, communications made in discharge of a public or private duty, either legal or moral, and anything written by a master in giving the character of a servant.[29] The Court also quoted, with approval, the view of "able judges" that candidates for office put themselves "in issue" so far as fitness or qualifications are involved.[30]

While the Supreme Court decision was not binding on state courts under the then interpretation of the Tenth Amendment to the United States Constitution, it often was cited by state appellate judges in later decisions. The national tribunal had enunciated a rule that privileged communications had to be proven malicious to be libelous, and that malice could be proved by showing falsity and lack of probable cause. This rule, as well as the standard allowing privilege for reports of official proceedings, could not be ignored. And while the decision in this particular case extended privilege to a letter written to an elected official about his servant, a customs official he appointed, it was only one step away from declaring privilege for publications circulated to people about their servants, officials they elected.

This far-reaching view served as a catalyst for change in America's civil law of libel. State after state, at first gradually and after the Civil War generally, extended some type of privilege to articles dealing with public officials and candidates.[31] And in the last quarter of the nineteenth century—when old values were being overturned and reassessed—judges in many states excused libelous falsehoods about officials and candidates when publications were made with proper cause for believing them true.[32] Others allowed damages to be mitigated on this basis.

Rulings, of course, varied with states. Some allowed privilege for only comment and criticism, not for misstatements of fact. Others allowed privilege for nonmalicious falsehoods about officials but required strict proof of truth for attacks on private character or for imputation of corrupt motives and misconduct.[33] But privilege was recognized only for discussion of those holding or seeking public office. It did not extend to libel of private individuals. Here truth had to be proved to justify a libel.[34] And in many states, truth had to be coupled with lack of malice. Some jurisdictions went further and required that truth be published with good motives for justifiable ends before a libel against a private individual could be excused.[35] There was, then, no uniform justification from state to state, in either libel of public or private individuals.

The territories of the United States presented still another facet of libel jurisprudence. And the Supreme Court shortly after the turn of the twentieth century upheld a criminal libel conviction of two Philippine editors even though they had been denied a jury trial. Under Philippine law, as approved by Congress, they had been tried before a judge for violating that territory's criminal libel statute. The Court said the right to trial by jury and other constitutional rights did not extend to the territories of the U.S. automatically, unless ordered by Congress, which was empowered by the Constitution to govern territories.[36]

The conviction in this 1904 case, *Dorr v. United States*, was upheld, though, because headlines over a story about a judicial proceeding—claiming a witness was a "traitor, seducer, and perjurer"—were found to be false, published "without basis, and wanton."[37] In rendering its decision, the Supreme Court pointed out that a fair and accurate report of a trial was privileged. Comments or remarks were not, the Court said, unless those comments were separate from the report itself and could be justified as fair comment and criticism.[38] The Court, then, was the final arbiter over territorial laws.

State law, though, was another matter. Whatever the individual state press policies were, the United States Supreme Court in the 1907 case of *Patterson v. Colorado* said they were matters of "local law" and could not be reviewed.[39] This case went to the Supreme Court on a test of the Fourteenth Amendment, which had been passed in 1868 at the close of the Civil War. One of the Fourteenth Amendment's provisions stated: "No state shall make or enforce any law which shall abridge the privileges or immunities of citizens of the United States; nor shall any State deprive any person of life, liberty, or property, without due process of law."[40] It was these words that the United States senator Thomas M. Patterson, publisher of the *Denver Times* and *Rocky Mountain News*, looked to when he was fined $1,000 for criticizing judges in his newspapers.

Patterson published an article and cartoon accusing the Colorado Supreme Court of participating in a fraudulent scheme to overturn an election won by a reform governor. The Colorado court held that the article was in contempt of court as it tended to interfere with the administration of justice in the election case, which technically was still pending in a suit for rehearing. Patterson, however, claimed that all that was involved was libel of judges, that he had a public duty to write truthfully of the judges, and that the state constitution provided the truth could be given in evidence in all cases of libel. To this, the Colorado court replied that contempt, not libel, was involved and that "the truth of published charges of corrupt motives . . . is no defense."[41] Patterson appealed to the United States Supreme Court, claiming that the Fourteenth Amendment prohibited the Colorado court from abridging privileges and immunities, and that freedom of the press was among the privileges and immunities guaranteed by the First Amendment.

The Supreme Court, however, found no constitutional issue that would warrant review. In a decision written by Justice Oliver Wendell Holmes, the Court said contempt extended to publications that embarrassed judges as well as to those interfering with the administration of justice. It added that truth was not a defense to contempt.[42] Then the Court sidestepped a ruling that the First and Fourteenth amendments were tied together. It issued the following dictum:

Even if we were to assume that freedom of speech and freedom of the press were protected from abridgements on the part not only of the United States but also of the states, still we should be far from the conclusions that the plaintiff in error would have us reach. In the first place, the main purpose of such constitutional provisions is "to prevent all such previous restraints upon publications as had been practiced by other governments," . . . and they do not prevent the subsequent punishment of such as may be deemed contrary to the public welfare. The preliminary freedom extends as well to the false as to the truth; the subsequent punishment may extend as well to the true as to the false. This was the rule of criminal libel apart from statute in most cases, if not in all.[43]

Only prior restraints, then, were considered by the Supreme Court of the United States to be invasions of press freedom. And reliance was placed on the old English common law, before the changes in American law and courts, for authority to punish both the true and false after publication.

Having effectively endorsed the constitutionality of postpublication sanctions, the Court next began to wrestle with the problem of when publications were actually libelous. The first of several such decisions came only two years later, in the 1909 case of *Peck* v. *Tribune.* And this decision, also rendered by Justice Holmes, set a precedent making it easier for people to obtain civil libel judgments against the press.

The case arose when the *Chicago Sunday Tribune,* an Illinois newspaper, published a testimonial advertisement for Duffy's Pure Malt Whisky. The advertisement contained a picture identified as that of Mrs. A. Schuman, stating she was a nurse and regularly used the whisky. But the picture actually was that of Mrs. Amanda Peck, an abstainer, a nurse, and a resident of Indiana near Chicago. She sued for libel, claiming the advertisement held her up to public hatred, contempt and ridicule. The case went to federal court because a resident of one state was suing a corporation of another state. The federal trial court ruled there was no libel, and this was sustained by the circuit court of appeals, which said there was no general consensus that to drink whisky was wrong. The Supreme Court, however, reversed the decision, saying that a libel does not depend on general consensus.

The Supreme Court decision said it was no excuse to claim a mistake was made or that another name appeared under the picture.[44] The publication of a picture coupled with a statement, the Court said, imports that the person in the picture made the statement. It was pointed out that people might recognize the face without knowing Mrs. Peck's name or that those knowing Mrs. Peck might conclude she had an alias.[45] Then the Court stated: "If the advertisement obviously would hurt the plaintiff in the estimation of an important and respectable part of the community, liability is not a question of majority vote. We know of no decision in which this matter is discussed upon principle. But obviously an unprivileged falsehood need not entail universal hatred to constitute a cause of action."[46] Strict liability, then, was the rule for published falsehoods about private individuals. The importance of the ruling, though, was that publications did not have to cause hatred, contempt and ridicule from all the public to be libelous. Publications could be libelous if they stimulated hatred, contempt or ridicule from only an "important and respectable part" of the public.

The public in the next case considered by the Supreme Court was that of Puerto Rico, and this time libel of an official, not a private individual, was involved. And the issue was privilege. The case began when a Puerto Rican newspaper, *La Correspondecia*, censured a United States district attorney in the territory, claiming his conduct was scandalous and immoral in serving as a public official while simultaneously acting as a private attorney for a party suing the government. The district attorney sued for libel, and the case, *Gandia* v. *Pettingill*, reached the United States Supreme Court in 1912.

The Supreme Court ruled that newspaper statements and comment did not go beyond the "permitted line" and was not excessive, as the acts were forbidden by law to Puerto Rican officials and were disapproved by the Puerto Rican community.[47] The Court also said the facts reported about the district attorney's private acts pertained to his conduct and acts in office. Then it ruled that "anything bearing on such acts was a legitimate subject of statement and comment. It was so at least in the absence of express malice."[48]

Though the Court had enunciated the "express malice" doctrine in *White* v. *Nicholls*, the 1845 decision on privileged communications, the *Gandia* v. *Pettingill* decision was the first in which the Court had specifically extended that doctrine to general newspaper discussion of public officials. And the opinion, written by Justice Holmes, made it clear that both factual statements as well as comment about officials were privileged so long as express malice was not proved.[49] And express malice, the Court had previously held, required proof of falsehood *and* publication without proper cause.

In fact, the Court in the 1913 case of *Nalle* v. *Oyster* reiterated the view that proof of falsity and lack of probable cause was required to show express malice. This suit arose after Mrs. Mary E. Nalle lost a court battle in which she attempted to force the District of Columbia School Board to rehire her as a teacher. She then filed a libel suit against the board because of a pleading the board had filed in the first case—to the effect that Mrs. Nalle was "deficient in the necessary academic and pedagogic equipment of a competent teacher." The libel action eventually went through the District of Columbia system and reached the Supreme Court, which ruled that the board's statement in the first trial was privileged when filed and had been sustained as true by the court judgment in that trial.

Hence, the Court said, there was no way for Mrs. Nalle to prove the statement was false and made without probable cause, which was necessary to show express malice.[50] The Supreme Court did make it clear, however, that pleadings in court, while privileged communications, were subject to libel sanctions if express malice were proved.

The only other issue considered by the Supreme Court before the end of World War I—and in two cases—was whether judges had power to declare statements libelous. The question in the first case was whether ambiguous words, not libelous in themselves, could be ruled by judges to be libelous in light of extraneous events. This, the Court said in the 1913 case of *Baker* v. *Warner,* did not fall within the province of judges. It was held instead that it was for the "jury and not the court to determine the meaning of ambiguous language in publication."[51]

This case resulted because Brainerd H. Warner, candidate for Congress, published an advertisement in a Washington newspaper asking if his opponent's campaign money was coming from the "race track." This infuriated Daniel W. Baker, United States district attorney for Washington, D.C., who was a close associate of Warner's opponent and who himself had been mentioned in the advertisement. The district attorney had been forced by court order to let a race track operate in the district, and he claimed the article imputed that he, as an associate of the candidate, was taking a payoff from the race track to let it remain open. The Supreme Court held, though, that there was no imputation of a payoff to the district attorney in the words themselves. Hence the article was not libelous per se as the trial judge had instructed. However, the meaning was ambiguous, the Court said, and a retrial was ordered to give the jury—not the judge—an opportunity to determine what the words meant.

A retrial also was ordered in *Washington Post Co.* v. *Chaloner,* decided just before the official end of World War I, in 1919. This case, too, held that if published words had more than one interpretation, the decision as to libel was that of the jury—not the judge. This case arose when the *Washington Post* carried an article stating that John Armstrong Chaloner had "shot and killed John Gillard, while the latter was abusing his wife, who had taken refuge at Merry Mills, Chaloner's home." Chaloner sued for libel and won a

$10,000 verdict in a District of Columbia court when the judge instructed the jury that the words implied murder had been committed by Chaloner. This verdict was overturned by the Supreme Court, which issued a writ of certorari for review.

In a decision written by Justice James C. Mc Reynolds, the Court said a statement to the effect that "C shot and killed G," by itself, was not libelous per se as it did not state in unambiguous langage that a crime had been committed.⁵² Further, the Court said, the added words, that the shooting occurred while Gillard was abusing his wife, "might at least suggest to reasonable minds that the homicide was without malice." The question as to fact hence was doubtful, the Court said, and doubtful questions of fact had to be determined by juries.

Summary

The Court, then, rendered several rather important libel decisions in the period that ended with World War I. It had held that jurors, not judges, determined the libelous import of ambiguous words and that publications could be libelous if considered so by only an "important and respectable part" of the public. Further it had said that a mistake could not excuse a libel and that the use of "false" and unauthorized pictures in advertisements may constitute libel. It had also ruled that fair and accurate reports of court trials, void of remarks and comments, were privileged. It recognized a privilege for separate fair comment and criticism. And the precedent-setting decision in *White* v. *Nicholls,* which said privileged communications were not libelous unless false *and* published without proper cause, was a forerunner of widespread state judgments that modified the civil law of libel.

From the Civil War to 1900—a period marked by a revolution in the social, cultural, and political life of the nation—state courts generally recognized a greatly expanded privilege to discuss public officials. Especial prominence was given to the new libel doctrine that excused falsehoods about candidates and holders of public office when publications were made in good faith and with proba-

ble cause for believing them true. With the perceived abuses of
yellow journalism, muckraking, and sensationalism in the early
twentieth century, however, a number of states began to back
away—either partially or completely—from such a privilege. Instead they often limited privilege to comment and criticism, not
factual misstatements.[53] But the Supreme Court continued in the
more liberal vein, holding in 1912 that scrutiny could be given to
the private acts affecting officials' conduct in office and that statements and comment about official conduct was legitimate "in the
absence of express malice."

Privilege, though, was extended only to suits involving actual and
would-be officials. In libel suits involving private individuals, the
only defense was truth. Such strict liability was required by the
Supreme Court, and in many states it was required that truth be
accompanied by good motives, and often that publications be for
justifiable ends.

Meanwhile, criminal libel prosecutions had gone into semihiber-
nation in the early nineteenth century, following the bitterness generated by the Sedition Law. The Supreme Court in the 1812 *Hudson and Goodwin* decision stated the federal government had no
power to prosecute for common law libel. Territories and states, of
course, could prosecute for criminal libel and continued to do so on
occasion.[54] But in state courts, too, there was a noticeable shift
from criminal to civil libel actions.

Further, it was clear after the 1833 decision in *Barron* v. *Mayor
of Baltimore* that these state decisions could not be reviewed by the
Supreme Court on the grounds that First Amendment guarantees of
press freedom had been violated. And in *Patterson* v. *Colorado,* in
1907, the Court refused to hold that freedom of the press was one
of the privileges and immunities protected from state infringement
by the Fourteenth Amendment. Supreme Court decisions were not
binding on the states in libel cases; state decisions were supreme. As
of World War I, the constitutional protection for free speech and
press had no force and effect in the various states. As the Supreme
Court itself said, in the immediate aftermath of the war: "Neither
the Fourteenth Amendment nor any other provision of the Constitution of the United States imposes upon the states any restriction
about 'freedom of speech.' "[55]

2/ Revised View of the Constitution
State Press Decisions Can Be Nullified

The philosophy of states' rights began to change rather rapidly after World War I, which had forced people to look to Washington, D.C., not their state capitals, for leadership. The war had brought national conscription, national price fixing, nationalization of the railways, and national control of utterances and publications considered disloyal.[1] And in the wake of the war, amendments to the United States Constitution nationalized the women's right to vote and instituted national Prohibition.[2] Nationalization was everywhere.[3] At first there was national prosperity but following the stock market crash of 1929, national depression. Then with Franklin D. Roosevelt's administration in 1932 came a national New Deal, accompanied by the National Industrial Recovery Act, the national Works Progress Administration and the national Social Security Act. It is no wonder, then, that in the midst of all this the Supreme Court of the United States nationalized the constitutional guarantees of free speech and press.

The old view of the Constitution, that it did not apply to state restrictions on press freedom, went by the wayside in 1925. The occasion came when Benjamin Gitlow, business manager of a radical newspaper, *Revolutionary Age,* appealed a New York conviction for publishing the "Left Wing Manifesto." The New York state courts had held that this violated the state Criminal Anarchy Act, and his appeal to the United States Supreme Court claimed the conviction violated his press freedom.

For the first time in history the Supreme Court ruled that it had the power to review state court decisions concerning the press to determine if freedom had been violated. In this landmark decision, *Gitlow* v. *New York,* the Court said it was "assumed" that freedom

15

of speech and press "are among the fundamental personal rights and liberties protected by the due process clause of the Fourteenth Amendment from impairment in the States."[4] The decision, though, did not help Gitlow. The Court balanced his right to advocate mass political strikes and militant revolution against New York's right to enforce a law to protect public peace and safety. It was ruled that his conviction, for subsequent and not prior restraint, was not an impermissible violation of press freedom.

The precedent had been set, however. The Supreme Court had assumed the right of oversight, through the Fourteenth Amendment, to review state press freedom cases. And the next case the Court considered, *Near* v. *Minnesota ex rel. Olson,* boldly stated that this right of oversight was "no longer open to doubt."[5] And in this case the Supreme Court overruled a state law, stating it was unconstitutional for Minnesota to place prior restraints on the publication of libels against public officials.

The case arose under what has been called the Minnesota Gag Law. It allowed the Minnesota courts to issue injunctions to suppress—as public nuisances—publications that regularly carried either "obscene, lewd and lascivious" or "malicious, scandalous and defamatory" publications.[6] For actions against defamatory publications, proof of truth, published with good motives and for justifiable ends, would be allowed in defense. Under this law, the county attorney in Minneapolis, Floyd B. Olson, in 1928 brought an action to enjoin the publication of the *Minneapolis Saturday Press.* Olson claimed the newspaper was "malicious, scandalous and defamatory."

At the trial, the publisher J. M. Near admitted publication, denied the articles were "malicious, scandalous and defamatory" as alleged, and claimed the state was violating his press freedom guaranteed by the Fourteenth Amendment. He refused to present other evidence. The court then ruled the publication to be malicious, scandalous, and defamatory. And he was permanently enjoined from producing his newspaper, under the title of *Saturday Press* or any other title. The law stipulated that if he violated the injunction, he could be punished for contempt of court, carrying a fine of up to $1,000 and/or one year in jail. When this verdict was upheld by the Minnesota Supreme Court, Near appealed to the United States Supreme Court with the assistance and financial backing of the *Chicago Tribune.*[7]

The Supreme Court in the 1931 *Near* v. *Minnesota ex rel. Olson* decision held that the action against the *Saturday Press* was the "essence of censorship,"[8] and thus "an infringement of the liberty of the press guaranteed by the Fourteenth Amendment."[9] This constitutional freedom from prior restraint was not lost because crimes were charged, the court said. Nor did it make any difference that the publisher was permitted a defense of truth, published with good motives for justifiable ends. If motives or justifiable ends were left to the discretion of legislators, the Court said, it would be but a "step to a complete system of censorship."[10] Further, it said the freedom from restraint before publication extended to the false as well as the true.

The Court also made it clear in the decision that it was not talking about all prior restraints being banned. Several areas were listed in which restraints are permissable before publication.[11] And a careful reading of the decision shows that dictum outlawing previous restraints dealt with libelous publications, particularly pertaining to "public officials" or "official misconduct." The Court even called attention to the fact that the decision was not "concerned with questions as to the extent of authority to prevent publications in order to protect private rights."[12] Yet the entire defamation section of the Minnesota Gag Law was overturned,[13] and this section allowed prior restraints for defamation against private individuals as well as public officials. The extent of the ban on prior restraints, then, was left somewhat muddled. But the result was that a state law to prevent publication of defamation was declared unconstitutional.

At its very narrowest interpretation, the holding left no doubt that prior restraints on libelous discussion of public officials violated the Fourteenth Amendment. It also left no doubt that state libel laws, civil and criminal, did not violate press freedom if they were consistent with constitutional privilege. The Court in this 5–4 decision, written by Chief Justice Charles E. Hughes, had this to say:

The fact that for approximately one hundred and fifty years there has been almost an entire absence of attempts to impose previous restraints upon publications relating to the malfeasance of public offices is signficant of the deep-seated convictions that such restraints would violate constitutional rights. . . . The fact that the liberty of the press may be abused by miscreant purveyors of scandal does not make any the less necessary the immunity of the press from previous restraint in dealing with official misconduct. Subsequent punishment for such abuses as may exist is the appropriate remedy, consistent with constitutional privilege.[14]

The Court did not even try to explain what was consistent with constitutional privilege in subsequent punishment. In fact, it stated specifically that "in the present case, we have no occasion to inquire as to the permissible scope of subsequent punishment."[15]

The dictum was clear, though, that the Court sanctioned both public and private redress by libel laws. Specifically, the Court said: "It is recognized that punishment for the abuse of liberty accorded to the press is essential to the protection of the public, and that the common law rules that subject the libeler to responsibility for the public offense, as well as for the private injury, are not abolished by the protection extended in our constitutions."[16] The only question left open concerning libel restraints, both before and after publication, was the limit placed on common law by "constitutional privilege," the scope of which was not an issue in the case.

Such privilege was an issue, however, in the next libel case the Supreme Court considered. The case resulted from a syndicated column, the "Washington Merry-Go-Round," published in a number of newspapers on 23 December 1938. It stated that Congressman Martin L. Sweeney opposed the appointment of a foreign-born Jew, Emerich Freed, as a judge of a federal district court. Sweeney sued at least sixty-eight different newspapers over the United States, seeking damages in excess of $7.5 million.[17] But in all but three trials—two in Illinois and one in New York—both federal and state courts declared the articles not libelous or protected by privilege.[18]

The New York decision, rendered by a federal circuit court of appeals on the basis of that state's law,[19] held that the article was false and libelous.[20] The column had been circulated in the *Schenectady Union Star* in an area of New York in which a number of Jewish people lived, and the court said this held the congressman up to hate and scorn before an important and respectable element of the community, the Jews who read the article. The circuit court's judgment was not unanimous, however. A dissenting opinion stated there should be no libel against public officials unless statements were both false and unfair and unless the aggrieved official proved special damages. On the basis of this dissent, the Supreme Court granted certiorari to review the decision.

The Supreme Court justices decided this case, *Schenectady Union Publishing Co.* v. *Sweeney* in 1941 on the eve of World War II, without Justice Robert H. Jackson taking part.[21] And they were equally divided as to whether the Constitution extended a libel-free privilege to nonmalicious falsehoods about public officials. As a result, the lower court decision was affirmed and the Supreme Court had missed an opportunity to render an opinion determining the constitutional limitations upon the power to award libel damages to public officials.[22]

Justices of the Supreme Court, then, like judges in the various states, were not agreed as to whether libel-free privilege should extend only to fair comment or to nonmalicious falsehoods as well. But there had been, between the two world wars, a growth in the number of states following the liberal rule that extended privilege to discuss officials to nonmalicious falsehoods, those published when there was probable cause for beliving them true. In fact, by the end of World War II, sixteen states had definitely adopted this view, and four other states and the District of Columbia had partially subscribed to it.[23] Meanwhile only twenty-one states and the territory of Hawaii could definitely be said to subscribe to the conservative view holding that fair comment and criticism were negated by false statements.[24] This conservative-liberal split concerning privilege was simply being reflected by Supreme Court justices in the *Sweeney* decision.

Strong differences of opinion also were voiced by the Supreme Court justices in the next libel decision, rendered in 1952 when Joseph Beauharnais invoked the Fourteenth Amendment to appeal a conviction from Illinois under a group libel law. This 5–4 decision, in *Beauharnais* v. *Illinois*, sanctioned the doctrine that states could penalize individuals for the crime of publishing hateful and libelous criticism of identifiable groups of people. Specifically, the decision upheld a $200 fine against Beauharnais, president of a White Circle League, for producing and circulating leaflets in Chicago asking "one million self-respecting white people" to unite against the Negro because of what he described as their "rapes, robberies, knives, guns and marijuana."[25] The leaflet also contained a petition for city officials to stop the "encroachment" of Negroes into the white neighborhoods.

The Illinois conviction was not under the common law but under a state statute that made it unlawful to publish or exhibit: "Any lithograph, moving picture, play, drama or sketch, which . . . portrays depravity, criminality, unchastity, or lack of virtue to a class of citizens, of any race, color, creed or religion to contempt, derision, or obloquy or which is productive of breach of the peace or riots."[26] On review, the United States Supreme Court classified the statute as a libel law for which there was common law precedent, said the leaflets were libelous, and held that libels were not protected by the First and Fourteenth amendments from state infringement.[27] The Court said that if a state could punish a libel directed at an individual, it could not be prohibited from punishing the same libel directed at a group "unless we can say that this is a wilful and purposeless restriction unrelated to the peace and well-being of the State."[28]

But the Court found the restriction was not purposeless. The majority opinion, written by Justice Felix Frankfurter, leaned heavily on the finding of the Illinois legislature that the words proscribed had a tendency to breach the peace. The legislative finding was not without reason, the opinion stated, in light of the racial strife, including riots, that had prevailed in the state. But the decision did not rest on this rationale alone. It also stated:

> It would . . . be arrogant dogmatism, quite outside the scope of our authority in passing on the powers of a State, for us to deny that the Illinois Legislature may warrantably believe that a man's job and his educational opportunities and the dignity accorded to him may depend as much on the reputation of the racial and religious group to which he willy-nilly belongs, as on his own merits. This being so, we are precluded from saying that speech concededly punishable when immediately directed as individuals cannot be outlawed if directed at groups with whose position and esteem in society the afflicted individual may be inextricably involved.[29]

Here, then, was recognition by the highest court in the land that the individual rights of group members were at issue in a group libel situation. The rationale for upholding the libel law was not restricted to disturbing the peace.

Though upholding this unique group libel law, the Court stipulated that "while this court sits it retains and exercises authority to nullify action which encroaches on freedom of utterance under the guise of punishing libel."[30] Four dissenters, however, felt it should have nullified the Illinois law. One dissenter, Justice Hugo Black, said pointedly that "state censorship" was involved when statements were punished that would have been praised in some parts of the United States. By extending criminal libel to include discussion of groups, he said, the majority gave criminal libel "a more expansive scope and more respectable status than it was ever accorded even in the Star Chamber."[31] He wondered aloud as to "how and when" the Court might protect the basic freedom of discussing matters of public concern.

There is no doubt that criminal libel laws in the states restricted discussion. And the Court's review in the *Beauharnais* decision showed that every state and territory at mid-century professed the right to punish scandalous and defamatory matter. Twenty-nine jurisdictions followed common-law precedents, the Court found, and twenty-three had specific libel statutes. All of the state statutes provided punishment for publications that blackened "the memory of one who is dead."[32]

From that point on, though, the Court found that the state statutes differed somewhat. They defined libel as being publications "tending to impeach the honesty, integrity, virtue or reputation" and/or "tending to expose one to public hatred, contempt, ridicule or financial injury" and/or "tending to deprive one of benefits of public confidence and social intercourse" and/or "exposing the natural defects of one who is alive."[33] Many of the common-law states also defined libel as including publications that aroused "scorn" or "obloquy," though the Court said other states had definitions that did not fall into common patterns. The Illinois statute on group libel definitely was not in the common pattern. In fact, it was not renewed by the Illinois legislature when the state's criminal statutes were revised in 1961. Further, the Supreme Court decision in *Beauharnais* v. *Illinois*, as one scholarly treatment states, "has neither been followed nor reversed."[34]

The next libel decision rendered by the Supreme Court, however, has of necessity been followed by all the states. This was the 1959 decision in *Farmers Educational & Cooperative Union of America,*

North Dakota Division v. *WDAY, Inc.,* which held that state libel laws do not apply to equal-time statements over the electronic media.[35] The decision, written by Justice Hugo Black, was made on the basis of federal law, not the Constitution. The Court said that station WDAY was not liable for defamation, regardless of state law, because the Federal Communications Act forced the station to allow the equal opportunity speech without power of censorship.

This was a turning point in the law of libel. For the first time in history, the Supreme Court had said a state could not invoke its libel laws to provide damages for an aggrieved party. And in doing so, it stressed the people's right to know about political affairs.

The case arose when a North Dakota candidate for the United States Senate, A. C. Townley, in a political speech over WDAY accused the Farmers Educational & Cooperative Union of America in North Dakota with conspiring to "establish a Communist Farmers Union." The union sued, but station WDAY claimed the provisions of section 315 (a) of the Federal Communications Act protected it from libel. The section of the law stated: "If any licensee shall permit any person who is a legally qualified candidate for any public office to use a broadcasting station, he shall afford equal opportunities to all other such candidates for that office in the use of such broadcasting station: *Provided,* That such licensee shall have no power of censorship over the material broadcast under the provisions of this section. No obligation is imposed upon any licensee to allow the use of its station by any such candidate."[36] The Supreme Court ruled that since the station could not control the candidate's speech, it could not be held responsible for it.

The Court said the purpose of the act was to stimulate full and unrestricted discussion of political issues by legally qualified candidates. Dictum read as follows:

Recognizing radio's potential importance as a medium of communication of political ideas, Congress sought to foster its broadest possible utilization by encouraging broadcasting stations to make their facilities available to candidates for office without discrimination, and by insuring that these candidates when broadcasting were not hampered by censorship of the issues they could discuss. Thus, expressly applying this country's tradition to the field of radio broadcasting, Congress has from the first emphatically forbidden the Commission to exercise any power of censorship over radio communication. It is in line with the same tradition that the individual licensee has consistently been denied "power of censorship" in the vital area of political broadcasts.[37]

With this decision, the electronic media was, in some respects placed in a preferred position so far as libel against officials and candidates were concerned. Only seven years before, in the *Beauharnais* case, the Court had ruled that state libel laws did not violate the United States Constitution. And the printed media still were subject to state libel laws.

There was with this decision, then, a double standard. Television and radio stations could not be held responsible for libelous statements in broadcast appearances by any candidate or official. Yet if newspapers or magazines printed these libelous statements, they did not have the same federal protection. This left them at a disadvantage. True, newspapers and magazines did not have the electronic media's legal responsibility to allow political rebuttals, but they nevertheless did have an ethical responsibility to print opposing views of candidates. And they also had a moral responsibility to provide competing voices in the marketplace of ideas.[38] Nevertheless, the print media were not afforded the libel-free protections this decision gave the competing electronic media for disseminating antagonistic views.

Additional disparity in the law of libel resulted from two other Supreme Court decisions in 1959. These decisions, *Barr* v. *Matteo* and *Howard* v. *Lyons,* gave public officials an immunity from libel not shared by common citizens. *Barr* v. *Matteo* resulted when several government employees claimed the acting director of the Office of Rent Stabilization had libeled them in a press release. But the Court ruled that Federal officials could not be held responsible for libel for any statements about their duties or the "outer perimeter" of their duties.[39] Officials, the Court stated, should be "free to exercise their duties unembarrassed by the fear of damage suits."[40] In *Howard* v. *Lyons*, the Court ruled that statements made by a military officer also were absolutely privileged.[41] A navy captain had been sued because he had voiced dissatisfaction, in an official report, about an employees' group at the Boston Naval Yard. The net effect of the two decisions, also written by Justice Black, was that federal officials could criticize citizens with an immunity to libel, but citizens had no similar immunity to criticize them.

Summary

The Supreme Court of the United States, then, had rendered decisions in 1959 that allowed a wide freedom of discussion, but on a select basis. Exclusions to the libel laws had been given to officials and to the broadcast media. But the Court in 1931 and 1952 had granted those using the printing press no exclusion whatsoever from either civil or criminal responsibility for libelous publications. The incongruity was striking.

It was just as incongruous that the Court should give an expansive scope to the law of criminal libel during a period marked by a "paucity of prosecutions" in this area.[42] Yet in the 1952 *Beauharnais* case, the Court sanctioned the punishment of those who published defamatory remarks about a "class of citizens," specifically racial or religious groups. The Court did rule, however, in the *Near* v. *Minnesota ex rel. Olson* case in 1931, that a state criminal statute to prevent publications of libel, specifically about public officials or official misconduct, was an unconstitutional prior restraint.

It was in the *Near* decision that the press won a most important victory. Here the Court said that the judicial review assumed for the purposes of the *Gitlow* case was no longer open to doubt, that the Fourteenth Amendment protected freedom of speech and freedom of the press from state impairment. These liberties, guaranteed by the First Amendment, were finally put under the safeguard of the Supreme Court, which with this decision clearly had oversight of state court judgments. Further, the Court said these judgments had to be consistent with the constitutional privilege of discussion. And in the *Beauharnais* case, the Court made a point to say it had authority to "nullify" libel decisions that encroached on that freedom of discussion.

The Court, then, was in a position to determine the law of libel for the entire nation. It missed an opportunity to do this, however, in the *Schenectady Union* case. The justices were evenly divided as to whether constitutional privilege to discuss public officials extended to nonmalicious falsehoods or only to fair comment and criticism. The division reflected a similar discord in state jurisdictions, though the liberal rule, allowing immunity for nonmalicious misstatements of fact, had gained wider acceptance. By the early 1960s, nineteen states granted a privilege for nonmalicious falsehoods about public officials, and three other jurisdictions partially subscribed to such a privilege.[43] Twenty-one states limited the libel-free privilege to fair comment and criticism about officials.[44]

The law of libel was being administered differently in different parts of the nation. Also it was being applied differently. One set of rules applied to the electronic media, and another set applied to the print media. Also public officials had an immunity from libel that private citizens did not have. Obviously there was a need for uniform administration and application of the laws of libel. But this could come only with a declaration of one law for all states, and such a declaration could come only from the United States Supreme Court.

3/ A New Constitutional Privilege
Libel Restricted by *New York Times* v. *Sullivan*

The Supreme Court of the United States on 9 March 1964, in an attempt to bring order and cohesion to the jurisprudence of libel, extended citizens everywhere a constitutional privilege to falsely defame public officials. The privilege, however, was conditional. As declared by the Court in the case of *New York Times* v. *Sullivan,* it existed only so long as the false libels were about officials' public conduct and were published without actual malice. And actual malice was defined as knowledge of falsity or reckless disregard of falsity.[1] The burden of proving the knowing or reckless falsehood, the Court said, was on the officials who brought damage suits for libel.

In effect, the Court had issued a new character of freedom to allow people to make misstatements of fact in even scandalous, contemptuous criticism of public officials. And the charter, based on free speech and press guarantees in the First Amendment to the United States Constitution, was made binding on the states through the Fourteenth Amendment.[2] It had to be enforced with uniformity and conformity in state and federal courts throughout the nation.

The new nationwide standard of libel propounded in *New York Times* v. *Sullivan* resulted from a full-page advertisement that the Supreme Court described as an "expression of grievance and protest on one of the major public issues of our time."[3] The *New York Times* advertisement, entitled "Heed Their Rising Voices," concerned the civil rights movement in Montgomery, Alabama, and asked the public to help Southern Negroes in their efforts to achieve human dignity. It said Negroes were being met with a "wave of terror by those who would negate the Constitution and the Bill of Rights." Several paragraphs were included to illustrate the wave of terror. And funds were requested to support Negro students in nonviolent protests, to help Negroes gain the right to vote, and to assist Dr. Martin Luther King, Jr., against a perjury indictment. It was signed by the "Committee to Defend Martin Luther King and the Struggle for Freedom in the South."[4]

It was claimed that two paragraphs in the advertisement had libeled the Montgomery commissioner of public affairs L. B. Sullivan, who supervised the police and fire departments. They read as follows:

In Montgomery, Alabama, after students sang "My Country 'Tis of Thee" on the State Capitol steps, their leaders were expelled from school, and truckloads of police armed with shotguns and tear-gas ringed the Alabama State College Campus. When the entire student body protested to state authority by refusing to reregister, their dining hall was padlocked in an attempt to starve them into submission.

. . . .

Again and again the Southern violators have answered Dr. King's peaceful protests with intimidation and violence. They have bombed his home almost killing his wife and child. They have assaulted his person. They have arrested him seven times—for "speeding," "loitering" and similar "offenses." And now they have charged him with "perjury"—a felony under which they could imprison him for ten years.[5]

Though Sullivan was never mentioned by name, he claimed that since he was in charge of the police department, he was accused of ringing the campus with police. Further, he said, the imputation was that police under his direction had padlocked the dining hall. He also claimed that the reference was to him, as police supervisor, when it said "they" had arrested Dr. King seven times, and that the "they" who arrested would be equated by readers with the "they" who bombed Dr. King's home and assaulted him. In effect, he claimed that he and police were accused of intimidation and violence in bombing Dr. King's home, in assaulting him, and in charging him with perjury.

To complicate the picture, many statements in the advertisement were inaccurate.[6] Students had not been expelled for the demonstration on the capitol steps but for demanding lunch-counter service at the Montgomery County Courthouse on a different day.

While most students protested the expulsion, it was not the entire student body. Nearly all the students reregistered, and the campus dining hall was never padlocked. Further, police had not been called for the capitol-steps demonstration. They had never ringed the campus. Dr. King had been arrested four times, not seven. And though he claimed to have been assaulted when arrested for loitering outside a courtroom, it had been denied by the officer making the arrest.

In alleging that he had been falsely and maliciously defamed, Sullivan asked libel damages of $500,000. He was awarded the full amount by an Alabama jury, and the judgment, the largest in the state's history,[7] was sustained by the Alabama Supreme Court. And for the first time in the history of this nation, the Supreme Court of the United States issued a writ of certiorari to review a state judgment in a civil libel suit.

Though there was precedent for the move,[8] the review was unusual. A private law suit was involved, not a state prosecution. And the Fourteenth Amendment guarantees only that states will not abridge citizens' privileges and immunities or deprive individuals of life, liberty, or property without due process of law. Of this, the Supreme Court in *New York Times* v. *Sullivan* stated: "Although this is a civil lawsuit between private parties, the Alabama courts have applied a state rule of law which petitioners claim to impose invalid restrictions on their constitutional freedoms of speech and press. It matters not that law has been applied in a civil action and that it is common law only, though supplemented by statute. . . . The test is not the form in which state power has been applied but, whatever the forms, whether such power has in fact been exercised."[9] A judge in rendering a civil libel judgment, then, was exercising state power. And state power could not be used to abridge freedoms guaranteed by the United States Constitution. This holding, which applied specifically to the *New York Times* case, had a much wider impact. In effect, any civil libel judgment in any state could be scrutinized by the nation's highest court to see that freedom was not abridged. This marked a major turning point in the jurisprudence of libel.

Another turning point came with the Court's decision that it made no difference that the allegedly libelous statements were in an advertisement. Previously it had been held that commercial advertisements were not protected by the Constitution.[10] The difference, the Court said, was that this paid advertisement was to discuss issues; hence it was protected by the Constitution. The opinion stated: "Any other conclusion would discourage newspapers from carrying 'editorial advertisements' of this type, and so might shut off an important outlet for the promulgation of information and ideas by persons who do not themselves have access to publishing facilities—who wish to exercise their freedom of speech even though they are not members of the press. . . . The effect would be to shackle the First Amendment in its attempt to secure the widest possible dissemination of information from diverse and antagonistic sources."[11] The only question at issue, the Court said, was whether the advertisement lost its constitutional protections because of false and allegedly libelous statements. Then it ruled that neither libel nor falsity nor a combination of the two was enough to forfeit those protections.[12]

In doing this, the Court refuted Sullivan's claims that libel was not protected by the Constitution.[13] It quoted the 1951 *Beauharnais* decision to the effect that authority was retained by the Court to "nullify action which encroaches on freedom of utterance under the guise of publishing libel."[14] The word *libel* carried no more weight than other labels of law,[15] the opinion stated, and effective criticism did not lose constitutional protection simply because it caused officials to lose their reputations.[16] Constitutional protections also were not limited to truth, the Court added, as erroneous statements were inevitable in free debate.[17]

Further, the decision stated that the lesson of the controversy over the Sedition Law of 1798 was that a combination of falsity and defamation was not sufficient "to remove the constitutional shield from criticism of official conduct."[18] It was added that the Sedition Act, which made it a crime to falsely libel government, had been shown by the "court of history" to be unconstitutional.[19]

The defense of truth allowed by the Sedition Law, and which was allowed in Alabama, was not a proper standard in libel suits filed by public officials, the Court said. There had to be an allowance for honest misstatement of facts. The opinion stated: "A rule compelling the critic of official conduct to guarantee the truth of all his factual assertions—and to do so on pain of libel judgments virtually unlimited in amount—leads to a comparable 'self censorship.' . . .

Under such a rule, would-be critics of official conduct may be deterred from voicing their criticism, even though it is in fact true, because of doubt whether it can be proved in court or fear of the expense of having to do so. . . . The rule thus dampens the vigor and limits the variety of public debate."[20] The Alabama rule of law applied in the *New York Times* case, then, did not provide the protection for the freedoms of speech and press which the Supreme Court of the United States felt was required by the First and Fourteenth amendments. Hence, the Alabama judgment was reversed.[21]

But the Supreme Court was not content with the simple reversal of the Alabama libel judgment. In this instance, it decided it should be a lawmaker as well as a law expounder.[22] The opinion, written by Justice William J. Brennan, Jr., specified that it was limiting the power of all states to award libel damages for statements about the official conduct of public officers.[23] The crux of the decision came in these words: "The constitutional guarantees require, we think, a federal rule that prohibits a public official from recovering damages for a defamatory falsehood relating to his official conduct unless he proves that the statement was made with actual malice—that is, with knowledge that it was false or with reckless disregard of whether it was false or not."[24] Noticeably, the holding was limited to defamatory statements about official conduct and did not apply to a public official's private life.[25] But if articles concerned their official conduct, public officials could not collect libel damages unless they proved publishers knew articles were false or that they recklessly disregard whether the articles were true or false. Further, the holding was not limited to publishers. The entire field of defamation—published libel and spoken slander—was covered. The constitutional privilege of nonmalicious discussion about officials was for everyone.

Still, the privilege granted under the new federal rule was conditional. And three Supreme Court justices, while basically agreeing with the majority decision, took exception to the conditions. Justice Arthur Goldberg, in his concurring opinion, stated there should be an "absolute, unconditional privilege to criticize official conduct despite the harm which may flow from excesses and abuses." In a separate concurrence, Justice Hugo Black stated the press should be granted an "absolute immunity for criticism of the way public officials do their duty."[26] Both opinions, which were subscribed to by

Justice William O. Douglas, stated the Constitution afforded an absolute right to discuss government affairs. Both opinions also expressed fear that the conditions—knowledge of falsity or reckless disregard of truth or falsity—would not stop future juries from awarding libel damages to officials.[27]

The majority opinion, however, served notice that the Supreme Court would review evidence independently of jury findings in similar suits, to assure there was no erroneous finding of malice.[28] While the Seventh Amendment to the Constitution prohibits any court from reexamining facts tried by juries, the Supreme Court said this did not mean that cases could not be reexamined to see if "governing rules of federal law have been properly applied to the facts."[29] And in reexamining the evidence in the *New York Times* case, the Court said that even if there were a new trial in Alabama, evidence lacked the "convincing clarity" which the Constitution required to support a libel judgment.[30]

The opinion stated that the "state of mind" required for the knowing or reckless falsehood was not in evidence.[31] In fact, there was no evidence whatever that those who authorized their names on the advertisement were aware of any erroneous statements or were reckless in any way.[32] And while the *Times* published the advertisement even through news stories in its files would have shown some of the statements to be false, the Court said this did not prove the newspaper personnel "knew" the statements were false.[33]

Further, the Court expressed the belief that normal—not reckless—procedures were followed in handling the advertisement.[34] It was routinely checked by the *Times*'s Advertising Acceptability Department, which found no personal attacks. Additionally, reliance was placed on the good reputation of the sponsors.[35] The lack of a retraction could not retroactively become evidence of malice for constitutional purposes, the Court said. And the testimony of the *Times*'s secretary at the trial that he still believed the advertisement was substantially correct, except for the padlocking accusation, was ruled not to indicate malice "at the time of publication."[36]

The Court, then, had shed light, to some extent, on the boundaries of its criteria for actual malice. It said: "The evidence against the Times supports at most a finding of negligence in failing to discover the misstatements, and is constitutionally insufficient to show the recklessness that is required for a finding of actual malice."[37] Recklessness was, then, something more than mere negligence. And the Supreme Court appeared to be saying that if there was no reason for believing statements false, there was no reckless disregard of falsity in not checking those statements.

Not only was there no reckless disregard of falsity in the publication, but the Court added one final touch by saying that in reality there was no libel against Mr. Sullivan. He originally had been awarded a libel judgment on a holding of the Alabama courts that criticism of governmental bodies reflected on those in control of those bodies. In attacking this holding, the Supreme Court said: "Raising as it does the possibility that a good-faith critic of government will be penalized for his criticism the proposition relied on by the Alabama courts strikes at the very center of the constitutionally protected area of free experession. We hold that such a proposition may not constitutionally be utilized to establish that an otherwise impersonal attack on governmental operations was a libel of an official responsible for those operations."[38] The Court held, in effect, that a public official cannot convert criticism of government into personal criticism for the purposes of a libel suit. Further the Court flatly said that prosecution for libel on government does not have "any place in the American system of jurisprudence."[39]

By holding that libel on government was contrary to American principles, the Supreme Court was not adding color to its decision. It was facing the issues involved. The case could not be separated from its reason for being. And that was an effort by a Negro minority to gain constitutional rights under a government by a white majority.[40]

What's more, there was evidence that Alabama was using its libel laws to suppress Negroes and their supporters in the civil rights movement. Sullivan, in suing the *New York Times* also had sued four of the eighty-four individuals who signed the published advertisement. Interestingly, the only four sued were Alabama Negro clergymen, including Dr. Martin Luther King's chief lieutenant, the Reverend Mr. Ralph D. Abernathy.[41] This assured jurisdiction in Alabama courts.[42] The $500,000 state libel judgment had been brought against all defendants, the newspaper and the clergymen. And an Alabama newspaper, the *Montgomery Advertiser*, carried a headline at the time stating that "State Finds Formidable Legal Club To Swing at Out-of-State Press."[43] This was no idle boast. When the Supreme Court overturned the *Sullivan* damage award, there already was another $500,000 libel judgment awarded to a second commissioner on the same advertisement. And Alabama officials had eleven additional libel suits pending against the newspaper for a total of $5.6 million.[44]

This was ample evidence that an attempt was being made to suppress discussion of Alabama government by making it appear that the discussion reflected on individual officials. Government libel was an issue as well as libel against officials. There is scant wonder, then, that the Supreme Court inserted these words in the *New York Times* v. *Sullivan* decision: "We consider this case against the background of profound national commitment to the principle that debate on public issues should be uninhibited, robust, and wide open, and that it may well include vehement, caustic, and sometimes unpleasantly sharp attacks on government and public officials."[45] While the issue in the case was libel, the foundation of the decision was the nation's commitment to freely discuss matters of public concern. And attempts to suppress this freedom had given birth to a new interpretation of the First Amendment that greatly expanded the right of all citizens to discuss public officials.

Summary

To see that First Amendment rights were protected, the Court for the first time, in *New York Times* v. *Sullivan,* utilized the Fourteenth Amendment to review a civil libel judgment. It also for the first time said constitutional protections extended to editorial advertisements. Again for the first time, it held that the Constitution protects both defamatory and false statements, and a combination of the two. The standard of the Sedition Law of 1798, that truth excused libel, was declared by the Court to be constitutionally insufficient. Defamed public officials, the Court said, had to prove actual malice—either knowledge of falsity or reckless disregard of falsity—when the defamation involved their official conduct.

Further, this proof had to be with convincing clarity. And the Court said it could and would review state libel decisions, independently of jury findings, to assure that constitutional standards were met.

In this decision, the Court gave the public a fair equivalent of the absolute immunity from libel previously granted in *Barr* v. *Matteo* to public officials in their discussions about their public duties.[46] However, the term *public official* was not defined in the decision, as the Court said it was unnecessary. And there was some ambiguity as to what had to be proved to show the knowing or reckless falsehood at the time of publication. But the Court made it clear it was not talking about negligence in not checking facts. Even negligent misstatements about officials were not actionable. The Court was talking about a tougher standard—a standard that it said was required by the United States Constitution. Under this standard, neither the communications media nor individuals could be held responsible in civil libel suits for nonmalicious falsehoods about the official conduct of public servants.

4/ An Expanded "Public-Official Rule" Limits Public Employee, Union, Criminal Libels

Only eight months after the revolutionary *New York Times* ruling, the Supreme Court, in the case of *Garrison* v. *Louisiana,* expanded the new constitutional privilege to discuss public officials. Here the Court said the same standards that protected individuals from civil libel judgments also protected them from criminal libel prosecutions. It added that even false and defamatory statements concerning *private* behavior that affected officials' public conduct were not subject to criminal sanctions without proof of actual malice—the knowing or reckless falsehood.[1] This was called the "public-official rule," and it was substituted for the then existing criminal libel laws in every state of the Union.

But while the "public-official rule" was conclusively defined, those to whom it applied were not. And the Court in early 1966, in the case of *Rosenblatt* v. *Baer,* said it would have to apply to some government employees as well as elected officials. Those employees thought by the public to have substantial responsibility for controlling government issues, the opinion stated, would have to prove the knowing or reckless falsehood to obtain a libel judgment.[2] Further, in a companion suit, *Linn* v. *United Plant Guard Workers of Americal Local 114*, the Court said individuals involved in union disputes would have to meet the same standard of proof—actual malice—before they, too, could receive any libel damages.[3] The Court obviously had used the *New York Times* decision as the foundation for building further constitutional protections for "uninhibited, robust, and wide open" debate.

The first of these "building" decisions, *Garrison* v. *Louisiana,* issued 23 November 1964, overturned a criminal libel conviction of the New Orleans district attorney Jim Garrison. He had been prosecuted because of angry accusations he made at a press conference about eight district judges in New Orleans. He accused them of taking overly long vacations, of laziness, of inefficiency, and of hampering his vice investigations by refusing to authorize his expenses. In addition, he questioned their personal motives in refusing the funds and said it raised "interesting questions about the racketeer influences on our eight vacation-minded judges."[4]

The Supreme Court, again in an opinion written by Justice William J. Brennan, Jr., said it made no difference that the Louisiana judges' private character had been impeached in the attack upon their performance of official duties. The opinion stated:

> Any criticism of the manner in which a public official performs his duties will tend to affect his private as well as his public reputation. The *New York Times* rule is not rendered inapplicable merely because an official's reputation is harmed. The public-official rule protects the paramount public interest in a free flow of information to the people concerning public officials, their servants. To this end, anything which might touch on an official's fitness for office is relevant. Few personal attributes are more germane to fitness for office than dishonesty, malfeasance, or improper motivation, even though these characteristics may also affect the official's private character.[5]

In effect, the Court said that an official's right to a good name is not as important as the public's right to know about him. Even charges of corrupt motives, dishonesty, or malfeasance did not lose their constitutional protection under the new "public-official rule."

What's more, the Court said the Constitution even protects discussion about the public conduct of officials that stems from hatred, anger, or ill will.[6] This was not "actual malice" as defined by the newly adopted "public-official rule," which totally prohibited truthful discussion of all types from being subjected to libel sanctions. Criminal or civil sanctions were possible, the Court said, only when public officials proved knowing or reckless falsehoods. With one declaration the Court had for all practical purposes wiped out criminal libel provisions in the fifty states and the District of Columbia. None of the then state statutes or common-law holdings measured up to the new rule.[7]

Further, under the new constitutional rule concerning public officials, the Court stated that "only those false statements made with a high degree of awareness of their probable falsity . . . may be the subject of either civil or criminal sanctions."[8] Stating also that the "calculated falsehood" was not protected by the Constitution, the Court added: "Although honest utterance, even if inaccurate, may further the fruitful exercise of the right of free speech, it does not follow that the lie, knowingly and deliberately published about a public official, should enjoy a like immunity."[9] The implication was that an official, to obtain a libel judgment, could prove a calculated falsehood or recklessness *only* when a publisher had a high degree of awareness of probable falsity.

It was not enough, the Court said, for an official to prove an individual did not have reasonable belief in the statements published. A lack of reasonable belief had been attributed to Garrison in his trial, and this prompted the Supreme Court to say that "the reasonable-belief standard . . . is not the same as the reckless-disregard-of-truth standard."[10] A showing that there was no reasonable belief would simply be a showing that ordinary care had not been taken, and the Court said: "The test which we laid down in *New York Times* is not keyed to ordinary care; defeasance of the privilege is conditioned, not on mere negligence, but on reckless disregard of the truth."[11] Even an individual who did not take ordinary care to determine whether statements were false, then, could not be held responsible for libel of public officials.

Without doubt, the Court in this decision had set several guidelines. First, constitutional protections went even to discussion of officials' private affairs that affected fitness for office. Second, officials could not obtain damages by proving that false and libelous statements were made without a reasonable belief in truth. And third, there had to be more than a normal awareness that statements were false, and recklessness was not mere negligence.

These new privileges to discuss public officials—as the Court pointed out in both *Garrison* v. *Louisiana* and *New York Times* v. *Sullivan* —were analogous to the immunity from actions for libel already enjoyed by public officials.[12] In each case the Court made the following statement: "It would give public servants an unjustified preference over the public they serve if critics of official conduct did not have a fair equivalent of the immunity granted to officials themselves."[13] In effect, the Court said, there was freedom for mutual criticism. And the Court quickly found occasion to re-express this view.

It came when the Mississippi Supreme Court upheld a libel judgment against Aaron E. Henry for accusing a county attorney and police chief of a "diabolical plot" in fabricating a charge of assault against a worker for the National Association for the Advancement of Colored People. Though the officials could lodge an official charge of assault, Henry's criticism of the charge was held libelous. But in 1965 the United States Supreme Court in *Henry* v. *Collins,* in a per curiam opinion, reversed this state judgment. The Court held that there was no showing that Henry made a knowingly false criticism or that he recklessly disregarded the truth.[14] Though the Court did not elaborate, it was made clear that the new federal rule of privilege indeed did correspond to the privilege that was enjoyed by officials. Mutual criticism had become more than a theory.

Also in *Garrison* v. *Louisiana* the Supreme Court had said the "modern consensus" was that criminal libel prosecutions were inappropriate for statements under which a civil libel suit could be maintained. Specifically, the Court stated: "Changing mores and the virtual disappearance of criminal libel prosecutions lend support to the observation that '. . . under modern conditions when the rule of law is generally accepted as a substitute for private physical measures, it can hardly be urged that the maintenance of peace requires a criminal prosecution for private defamation.' "[15] The Court also quoted the American Law Institute's Proposed Official Draft of the Model Penal Code to the effect that there should be only narrowly drawn criminal libel statutes designed to punish words that would cause "harmful behavior which exceptionally disturbs the community's sense of security."[16] An example given was group villification, "especially likely to lead to public disorders," such as the statute sustained in *Beauharnais* v. *Illinois* in 1951.

The implication was clear. Criminal libel actions should not be substituted for civil law suits and should be used only against speech or publications likely to cause major breaches of the peace. In determining when words tended to breach the peace, the Court further said that the clear-and-present danger standard was relevant.[17] The Court said that the Louisiana statute, used against Garrison, was not narrowly drawn to meet modern day standards.

The *Garrison* case, then, set the stage for the Supreme Court's decision in early 1966 that Kentucky's broad criminal libel statute was unconstitutional.[18] In this decision, *Ashton* v. *Kentucky,* the Court was faced with a Kentucky state court conviction of a labor agitator for a libel described as a "writing calculated to create disturbance of the peace." The agitator, Steve Ashton, had published a pamphlet accusing Hazard, Kentucky, law enforcement officials of deputizing mine operators to stop a mining strike and, in the resulting disturbances, of blinding a boy. The pamphlet also accused the newspaper publisher in Hazard of withholding money and food sent to strikers, in care of the newspaper, from all over the nation. At the trial, Ashton was found guilty, fined $3,000, and sentenced to jail for six months.

The Supreme Court on review, however, overturned the conviction along with Kentucky's vague criminal libel law, which did not define what type of publications caused breaches of the peace. The opinion stated: "To make an offense of conduct which is 'calculated to disturbances of the peace' leave wide open the standard of responsibility. It involves calculations as to the boiling point of a particular person or a particular group, not an appraisal of the comments *per se.* This kind of criminal libel 'makes a man a criminal simply because his neighbors have no self-control and cannot refrain from violence.' "[19] The Court said that when a First Amendment right was involved, as here, the law had to be very carefully and narrowly drawn to require an appraisal of the publication itself.[20] As the criminal law had not been redefined in Kentucky—as in many other states—it was held that it should not be enforced as a penal offense.

Actually, at the time of the Kentucky prosecution, there was no other way a labor agitator or anyone else involved in a union dispute could have been brought into court for publishing an alleged libel. Civil suits for libel were prohibited in labor disputes by the National Labor Relations Act, which assured uninhibited exchanges between labor and management.[21] However, the Supreme Court opened the door for civil libel suits in these disputes early in 1966, in the same year it issued the *Ashton* v. *Kentucky* decision.

The occasion came in *Linn* v. *United Plant Guard Workers of America Local* 114.[22] This was a case brought in state court by a Pinkerton Detective Agency official, William C. Linn, against a union of Pinkerton employees because of leaflets distributed in a labor dispute. The leaflets stated Linn had lied to employees and robbed them of pay increases. He claimed this falsely defamed him. On review, to determine if the action could stand, the Supreme Court said society had a deep interest in protecting reputation and that state civil libel remedies were appropriate, even during a union organizing campaign. But individuals bringing such libel actions, the Court said, would have to follow the public-official rule and prove knowing or reckless falsehoods before damages for actual injury could be awarded.

The messages of the *Linn* and *Ashton* cases, then, appeared to be that private libel in labor disputes required civil action, not criminal prosecution, *and* proof of actual malice. While one might argue that a publication in a labor dispute could cause harmful behavior disturbing a community's security, states were put on warning in *Ashton* that criminal statutes had to be narrowly drawn to conform to constitutional guarantees of free discussion. And the constitutional guarantees were interpreted to give individuals a libel-free privilege—short of the knowing and reckless falsehood—in labor dispute discussions as well as in discussions of public officials.

This libel-free privilege established by the Supreme Court, however, still left a major question unexplored. It was the question as to who was a public official, as to who could be discussed with the latitude allowed by *New York Times* v. *Sullivan* and *Garrison* v. *Louisiana.* One of these cases had been filed by an elected city commissioner, and the other was a prosecution for statements pertaining to district judges. All were without doubt public officials. Nevertheless, clear lines had not been drawn as to the extent of the "public official" designation.

A line was drawn by the Supreme Court in *Rosenblatt* v. *Baer,* decided also in early 1966. Here it held that the term *public official* was not limited to elected officials alone. The Court said public officials included governmental employees, at least those believed by the public to have substantial responsibility for governmental affairs.[23]

The case arose because of a newspaper column written by Alfred D. Rosenblatt about a public ski resort in New Hampshire. At the time he wrote the column, the resort was operated by the state. But six months previously, Frank P. Baer was the appointed supervisor, being directly responsible to three elected county commissioners. The column claimed there had been a huge increase in the resort income under the new state management. It further asked what had happened to "all the money last year? and every other year?" and wondered what "magic" the new managers had performed. On the strength of these statements, Baer sued for libel and obtained a $31,500 judgment. After the judgment and before the New Hampshire court affirmed it, the *New York Times* decision was issued. And it was on the principles of that decision that the Supreme Court of the United States granted certiorari.

At the outset, the Supreme Court stated that Rosenblatt's column was in itself no more than an "impersonal discussion of government" and contained no clearly libelous statement.[24] It was not enough, the Court said, for Baer to prove a large part of the community understood the column to charge dishonest manipulation of funds at the governmentally operated resort. The opinion, still another written by Justice Brennan, stated: "A theory that the column cast indiscriminate suspicion on the members of the group responsible for the conduct of this governmental operation is tantamount to a demand for recovery based on libel of government and therefore is constitutionally insufficient."[25] The Constitution, the Court said, "does not tolerate" libel on government.[26] And Baer, who was responsible to the three county commissioners, could not be libeled—whether a public official or not—unless he showed evidence that the column was made "specifically of and concerning him."[27] On this basis alone the case was reversed.

The question still remained, however, as to whether Baer, in his position as a public ski resort supervisor, was really a public official. And the Supreme Court had asked the attorneys of both sides to brief and argue this point. The purpose clearly was to establish a national, uniform standard for defining the term *public official*. The Court specifically stated that individual state definitions for "officials" were insufficient as there could be no state jurisdictional variance on the limits of constitutionally protected expression.[28]

In setting a uniform standard, the Supreme Court said that to assure uninhibited debate on public issues, the "public-official rule" would of necessity have to apply to individuals in a position to influence the settlement of those issues. More specifically, the Court held: "The 'public official' designation applies at the very least to those among the hierarchy of government employees who have, or appear to the public to have, substantial responsibility for or control over the conduct of government affairs."[29] A precise line, then, was not drawn by the Supreme Court. Some clarity, however, was added by a footnote to the opinion, which stated: "The employee's position must be one which would invite public scrutiny and discussion of the person holding it, entirely apart from the scrutiny and discussion occasioned by the particular charges in a controversy."[30] In effect, a publication, broadcast, or discussion could not in itself make a "public official" out of an employee. His position would have to be such as to invite independent scrutiny. But the definition did include employees as well as elected officials, and it did provide a guideline for judges in all states and federal jurisdictions.

Moreover the Court made it clear that judges, and not jurors, were to determine if employees of government were public officials. It stated: "As is the case with questions of privilege generally, it is for the trial judge in the first instance to determine whether the proofs show respondent to be a 'public official.' "[31] As the Court put it, the determination by judges would lessen the possibility that juries "will use the cloak of a general verdict to punish unpopular ideas or speakers."[32] And it would assure a proper record of the findings in case of a review of constitutional principles. Additionally it opened the door for speakers and publishers sued by officials to seek summary judgments to stop the high cost of trials.

So far as Baer was concerned, the Supreme Court said there was a "substantial argument" that he came under the "public-official rule" since he had claimed in his suit that the public regarded him as responsible for its resort operations.[33] However, the Court did not make the final decision. The issue was sent back to New Hampshire for retrial because the case originally was tried before the *New York Times* decision.[34] Also in the original trial, Baer had proved only that Rosenblatt's column contained negligent misstatements of fact. The Supreme Court stated that if Baer was found in a new trial to be a public official, it would not be enough to prove negligence or lack of ordinary care.[35] He would have to prove that the column was published with knowledge of falsity or with reckless disregard of whether it was true or false. Even if he proved he was not a public official, he still would have to show that he had been libeled.

This was the first of the rapid-fire public-official libel decisions since *New York Times* v. *Sullivan* in which all justices did not concur. A complete dissent was lodged by Justice Abe Fortas on the ground that the writ of certiorari should not have been granted as the trial came before the *New York Times* decision.[36] Then there was a division of thought as to Baer's status. Justices William O. Douglas and Hugo L. Black, for instance, concurred as to the reversal but dissented as to the retrial. Both said there should be no limit on discussion as to the way any agent of government does his job.[37] A dissent on the portion of the opinion that dealt with impersonal libel came from Justice John Marshall Harlan. The Rosenblatt column, he said, was not aimed at such a wide group as the "police" that had been cited in the Sullivan case. He felt it was aimed at a group so small that a jury could legitimately make a direct connection to Baer.[38] And Justice Potter Stewart wrote a separate concurring opinion in which he cautioned that the *New York Times* rule did not apply to libel of private citizens.[39]

The majority opinion, however, did not close off the possibility that private citizens might fall under the *New York Times* rule. Following a statement that the Constitution limits libel laws when "interests in public discussion are particularly strong" and an employee's position in government triggers that interest, The Court appended a footnote stating: "We are treating here only the element of public position, since that is all that has been argued and briefed. We intimate no view whatever whether there are other bases for applying the *New York Times* standards—for example, that in a particular case the interests in reputation are relatively insubstantial, because the subject of discussion has thrust himself into the vortex of the discussion of a question of pressing public concern."[40] Here was an indication that the constitutional privilege of discussion might not be limited to public officials. In fact, the Supreme Court's definition of a public official in *Rosenblatt* v. *Baer* was grounded on the thesis that the public should have wide freedom to discuss those in positions to influence the resolution of public issues.[41]

Summary

The common denominator in all of these Supreme Court decisions—*Rosenblatt* v. *Baer, Linn* v. *United Plant Guard Workers of American Local 114, Ashton* v. *Kentucky, Henry* v. *Collins* and *Garrison* v. *Louisiana*—was the right to discuss public issues. *Rosenblatt* involved statements critical of operations at a public ski resort. *Linn* involved rough discussion in a labor dispute. *Ashton* resulted from a publication about communitywide strike activities, and *Henry* dealt with criticism of a public prosecution. Further, *Garrison* focused on heated discussion concerning a thwarted vice investigation. And in each of the decisions, the Court had contributed to enlarging the freedom of discussion while reducing the area of libel.

These libel decisions, the progeny of *New York Times* v. *Sullivan,* primarily dealt with public officials. And the Court said that public officials included governmental employees believed by the public to have substantial responsibility for governmental affairs. These officials not only had to prove actual malice—the knowing or reckless falsehood—to collect libel damages for defamatory falsehoods about their *official conduct* but also had to make the same proofs even when statements were made with hatred or ill will about their *fitness for office.* Discussion of their private reputation also was protected by the Constitution.

The Court explained the constitutional protection by saying proof that there was knowledge of falsity required a showing of a calculated falsehood. And recklessness could not be proved by showing lack of ordinary care or negligence, such as when the speaker or publisher had no reasonable belief in the truth of statements made. The Court was not talking about the same belief-in-truth doctrine of privilege that arose after the Civil War and that had so sharply divided the courts of the nation. It was talking about a new Constitution-granted privilege that required a more than normal awareness of falsity before recklessness could be proved. Further, the Constitution, the Court said, did not sanction any libel on government. Hence officials had to prove that any governmental discussion was "of and concerning" them before any successful libel action could be taken. And the Court said all these standards applied in criminal libel actions as well as civil suits.

Notice also was served that criminal libel statutes had to be narrowly drawn to meet the new constitutional standards. In this respect, the Court said it was the consensus that criminal prosecutions should not be used when personal libel was at issue. And it strongly indicated that criminal libel laws should be reserved for those instances when speech or publication created a clear and present danger of causing breaches of the peace. Further, the Court ruled that criminal libel laws could not be gauged on the "boiling point" of readers or listeners. It had to be gauged from the publication itself. As a result of these decisions, some state supreme courts later were forced to overturn their state laws on criminal libel.[42] Still others did not redraft their laws, and one authority said the criminal libel area was "clearly dying."[43]

It also appeared for a period after these decisions that successful libel suits by public officials were dying. Prior to 1968, when it became evident that this was not so, only two cases were reported in which officials were able to sustain judgments in state appellate courts.[44] The "public-official rule" was rapidly assimilated into state law as both state and federal jurisdictions modified their old doctrines of libel to conform to the new constitutional privilege. Cases were heard in these lower courts in which the public official designation was applied to all types of individuals connected to government.[45] Among them were an architect on a public building, an owner of a private garbage collection agency serving a city, and the operators of a nursing home licensed by a state.[46] Even a college student serving as a student senator was declared a "public official" when bringing a libel suit against the student newspaper.[47]

In some instances, even private individuals falsely defamed when involved in routine government affairs were unable to obtain libel judgments unless they, too, followed the "public-official rule" and proved actual malice—knowledge of falsity or reckless disregard of falsity.[48] Even the Supreme Court had held in *Linn* that actual malice had to be proved by private individuals when libel suits resulted from union disputes. The impact of the Court-granted constitutional privilege had quickly moved beyond the discussion of public officials, and it was noticeable. Several lower courts, for example, held that public figures as well as public officials had to prove actual malice in libel cases.[49] An obvious liberalizing of libel laws had taken hold. Courts generally had accepted the Supreme Court's footnoted remark that there might be "bases" other than public officials for applying the *New York Times* standard in the discussion of public affairs.

5/ Privilege to Discuss Public Figures
Libels Bound by Public-Official Rule

The rationale behind the United States Supreme Court decisions limiting libel judgments for public officials had been the nation's commitment to "uninhibited, robust, wide open" debate on public issues. Such a rationale could easily be given expansive interpretation, and this is exactly what happened in lower and federal courts.[1] Even the Supreme Court, in *Rosenblatt* v. *Baer,* had hinted at a readiness to expand the public-official rule—to those who thrust themselves into the vortex of discussions on matters of public concern.[2] The Court, however, did not face this issue squarely until June 1967, in the cases of *Associated Press* v. *Walker* and *Curtis Publishing Co.* v. *Butts.* In these cases, decided simultaneously, the Court held by a 5–4 margin that public figures as well as public officials could collect libel damages only by proving that defamatory falsehoods about them were made with knowledge of falsity or reckless disregard of whether they were true or false.[3]

The *Associated Press* and *Curtis Publishing Co.* decisions, though, did not occur in a void. Only four months before, the Supreme Court had applied the public-official rule to another, but related, area of law. It had ruled in *Time, Inc.,* v. *Hill* that constitutional standards had to be met before damages could be awarded to a private individual for invasion of privacy resulting from false reports on matters of public interest. The standards required, the Court said, proof that publications were made with knowledge of falsity or with reckless disregard of the truth.[4] Though non-defamatory falsehoods were involved, the same constitutional privilege of discussion applied. And it applied to a discussion of a private individual in a magazine article about a matter of public concern.

The article, in *Life* magazine, was entitled "True Life Crime Inspires Tense Play" and told of the opening of a play on Broadway in 1955. It said the play was inspired by the experiences of James Hill and his family, who three years earlier had been held hostage by escaped convicts in their home near Philadelphia. While the incident did give the author his idea for the play, he wrote a fictitious account about a "Hilliard" family. And the play differed from reality. In real life, the Hills were not harmed or badly treated by the convicts. But the play of the Hilliards showed the father and son being beaten and the daughter receiving a "verbal sexual insult."[5] And the idea promoted in the *Life* article was that the play reenacted the Hill experiences, and people could learn how "a family rose to heroism in a crisis."[6] The accompanying pictures showed actors performing scenes in the old Hill home, depicting the father with a gun, the son being "roughed up," and the daughter biting the hand of a convict.

Obviously there was no injury to the Hills' reputation in the fictionalized account—and no basis for a libel suit. Hill, however, said the article placed him and his family in a "false light" while invading their privacy. He sued in New York courts under the New York privacy act and eventually won a $30,000 damage award. *Life*'s parent company, Time, Inc., appealed to the Supreme Court on the basis that freedom of the press had been infringed by the state judgment.

The Supreme Court agreed. Pointing out that the subject of the article, a play tied to an actual event, was a matter of public interest,[7] the opinion stated: "The guarantees for speech and press are not the preserve of political expression or comment upon public affairs, essential as those are to healthy government."[8] Further, it said that errors would be common in all types of public interest discussion and that those errors must be protected when innocent or merely negligent.[9] Hill would have to go through another trial, the Court said, to prove a knowing or reckless falsehood to obtain damages. This he never did.[10]

The Court made it clear that it was applying the *New York Times* public-official libel rule in the "particular context" of private individuals suing for invasion of privacy stemming from discussion of public issues.[11] It stated specifically that if a public official had been involved in such a privacy action, "a different test might be required."[12] Also the Court said if libel had been involved, the "discrete context" of the Hill case would change as "additional state interest in the protection of the individual against damage to his reputation would be involved."[13] Libel of private individuals, then, was another matter.

From a libel standpoint, perhaps the major significance of this case, at this time, was the specific declaration by the Supreme Court that constitutional protection extended to false discussion of public issues that are not governmental issues. This being the case, it stood to reason that the Constitution also should protect, to some extent, discussion about individuals other than public officials who could influence public issues. And two such individuals were involved in the 1967 libel cases of *Curtis Publishing Co.* v. *Butts* and *Associated Press* v. *Walker*. The two individuals, Wallace Butts and Edwin A. Walker, had greatly differing backgrounds. Each, though, commanded continuing public interest and influence over matters of general concern.

Butts was the athletic director at the University of Georgia, with overall responsibility for that university's athletic program. He was particularly well known in football circles at the time the *Saturday Evening Post* published, on 23 March 1963, an article entitled "The Story of a College Football Fix." The story was based on a telephone conversation which an Atlanta insurance salesman, then on probation on a hot check charge, had been "cut into" because of an electronic error. The article was preceeded by a note from the editors as follows: "Not since the Chicago White Sox threw the 1919 World Series has there been a sports story as shocking as this one. . . . Before the University of Georgia played the University of Alabama . . . Wally Butts . . . gave to its coach . . . Georgia's plays, defensive patterns, all the significant secrets Georgia's football team possessed."[14] The article then told of the 1962 Georgia-Alabama game, listed players' reactions, and stated that "Georgia players, their moves analyzed and forecast like those of rats in a maze, took a frightful physical beating."[15]

The article also told of Butts's resignation for health and business reasons after the insurance man, George Burnett, gave his notes of the telephone conversation to the Georgia head coach. Butts, who was employed as athletic director by the Georgia Athletic Association and not by the state, had been negotiating at the time for a position with a professional team.[16] The article stated: "The chances are that Wally Butts will never help any football team again. . . . the investigation by university and Southeastern Conference officials is continuing; motion pictures of other games are being scrutinized; where it will end no one so far can say. But careers will be ruined, that is sure."[17] Before this article was published, Butts and his daughter notified the *Saturday Evening Post* that it was false.[18] But when the article was published anyway, he sued for libel in federal court, claiming that he had been falsely accused of "fixing" the game and that the magazine's conduct was reckless and wanton.

At the trial, evidence showed that Burnett had overheard a conversation, but what was said in that conversation was "hotly disputed."[19] Also expert witnesses who saw the notes and game films supported Butts's contention that the conversation was general football talk. Player's remarks published in the *Post* were severely contradicted. The result was a jury award of $60,000 in general damages and $3 million in punitive damages. This was reduced by the court to $460,000 total.[20]

While Butts's case stemmed from published discussion of college sports, Walker's resulted from published discussion of college riots at the University of Mississippi, occasioned by the federally-enforced enrollment of the university's first Negro. Walker, a retired major general in the United States Army, had considerable political prominence as a Southern Conservative and opposed the forced integration. During the week before the riots, in 1962, he had made several radio and television appearances in which he urged defiance of court orders and federal power.[21] On the night of the riots, he was on the university campus, and he was discussed in a story dispatched by a twenty-one-year-old Associated Press correspondent. Under the by-line of Van Savell, the story said, in part:

Oxford, Miss., Oct. 3 (AP)—Utilizing my youth to the fullest extent, I dressed as any college student would and easily milled among the several thousand rioters on the University of Mississippi Campus Sunday night.

This allowed me to follow the crowd—a few students and many outsiders—as they charged federal marshals surrounding the century old Lyceum Building. It also brought me into direct contact with former Maj. Gen. Edwin A. Walker. . . .

One unidentified man queried Walker as he approached the group. "General, will you lead us to the steps?"

I observed Walker as he loosened his tie and shirt and nodded "Yes" without speaking. He then conferred with a group of about 15 persons who appeared to be the riot leaders.

The crowd took full advantage of the near-by construction sticks and broken soft drink bottles.

Walker assumed command of the crowd, which I estimated at 1,000.

Walker, who himself had commanded army units that enforced integration at Central High School in Little Rock, Arkansas, only five years before, denied that he took part in any charge against federal marshals. He said he had counseled peaceful protest and claimed the article falsely accused him of leading a charge of students and of assuming command of the crowd.

As a result of the article, Walker filed a series of libel suits against newspapers carrying the AP article, in which he asked total damages of $33,250,000.[22] While these were in various stages of completion, he won a jury verdict against the Associated Press in Texas courts. The Texas jury awarded him $500,000 compensatory damages and $300,000 punitive damages, but the trial judge eliminated the punitive damages because there was no evidence of actual malice. The trial judge said "negligence, it may have been; malice it was not."[23] This reduced verdict of $500,000 in compensatory damages was upheld on appeal to the Texas Court of Civil Appeals.

Walker's state court judgment and Butts's federal court judgment went to the United States Supreme Court on grants of certiorari because of the New York Times v. Sullivan decision concerning freedom to discuss public issues. As stated in the opinion of Justice John Marshall Harlan, the Court wanted to review the cases "to consider the impact of that decision on libel actions instituted by persons who are not public officials, but who are 'public figures' and involved in issues in which the public has a justified and important interest."[24] It was pointed out that state courts and lower federal courts were sharply divided as to whether the New York Times rule applied to other than public officials.[25] Hence the Court said it needed to clarify the relationship between libel law and freedom of speech and press.[26]

An accommodation had to be found, Harlan's opinion stated,

between libel law, designed to protect society's interest in "preventing and redressing attacks upon reputation," and society's other interest in free public discussion.[27] Additionally the opinion quoted *Time, Inc.,* v. *Hill* to the effect that "guarantees for speech and press are not the preserve of political expression." The intent of the Founders, it stated, was that a free press would advance "truth, science, morality and the arts in general."[28] Hence criticism of private citizens in positions to lead in the determination of policy would have to be considered no less important to public interest than criticism of "public officials."[29] Butts and Walker were considered to be private citizens in such positions. As a result they were declared "public figures"—Butts because of his "position alone" and Walker because he had thrust "his personality into the vortex of an important public controversy."[30] And the Court said "public figures" would have to meet constitutional standards rather than the less demanding state standards in obtaining libel judgments.[31]

Up to this point the justices of the Supreme Court were united. But they were divided on the constitutional standard that should be adopted in protecting discussion about public figures. All would have protected false and defamatory statements about public figures to some extent.[32] But four of the justices, whose views were expressed in Justice Harlan's lead opinion, would have stopped that protection "on a showing of highly unreasonable conduct constituting an extreme departure from standards of investigation and reporting ordinarily adhered to by responsible publishers."[33] Chief Justice Earl Warren, however, called this an "unusual and uncertain formulation" and rejected it as inadequate for "the protection for speech and debate that is fundamental to our society and guaranteed by the First Amendment."[34]

Warren's view on this, expressed in a one-man pivotal opinion, was endorsed by the four remaining justices in still other opinions.[35] Speaking, then, for a five-member majority of the Court, he asserted that separate constitutional standards for public figures and public officials had "no basis in law, logic, or First Amendment policy." He then said:

I therefore adhere to the *New York Times* standard in the case of "public figures" as well as "public officials." It is a manageable standard, readily stated and understood, which also balances to a proper degree the legitimate interests traditionally protected by the law of defamation. Its definition of "actual malice" is not so restrictive that recovery is limited to situations where there is a "knowing falsehood" on the part of the publisher of false and defamatory matter. "Reckless disregard" for the truth or falsity, measured by the conduct of the publisher, will also expose him to liability for publishing false material which is injurious to reputation. More significantly, however, the *New York Times* standard is an important safeguard for the rights of the press and the public to inform and be informed on matters of legitimate interest. Evenly applied to cases involving "public men"—whether they be "public officials" or "public figures"—it will afford the necessary insulation for the fundamental interests which the First Amendment was designed to protect.[36]

The so-called public-official rule had been expanded by the majority of the Court. The impact of the decision was that public figures as well as public officials would be required to prove actual malice—the knowing or reckless falsehood—to collect libel damages.

The rationale presented in the Warren opinion for this expansive interpretation of the public-official rule was important. The opinion pointed out that power had increased in the "private sector" as well as in government since the depression of the 1930s. Then it stated:

In many situations, policy determinations which traditionally were channeled through formal political institutions are now originated and implemented through a complex array of boards, committees, commissioners, corporations and associations, some only loosely connected with the Government. This blending of positions and power has also occurred in the case of individuals so that many who do not hold public office at the moment are nevertheless intimately involved in the resolution of important public questions or, by reason of their fame, shape events in areas of concern to society at large.

Viewed in this context, then, it is plain that although they are not subject to the restraints of the political process, "public figures," like "public officials," often play an influential role in ordering society. . . . Our citizenry has a legitimate and substantial interest in the conduct of such

persons, and freedom of the press to engage in uninhibited debate about
their involvement in public issues and events is as crucial as it is in the case
of "public officials."[37]

Individuals who by fame or involvement were in positions to shape
issues or events of concern to society, then, were seen as subject to
free discussion, short of the knowing or reckless falsehood. The
opinion further stated that the public opinion generated by this
discussion might be the "only instrument by which society can
attempt to influence" the conduct of such public figures.[38]

In looking at the conduct of Walker, and the Associated Press
article concerning him, the Court unanimously agreed that the
$500,000 libel judgment had to be reversed. "Under any reasoning,
General Walker was a public man in whose public conduct society
and the press had a legitimate and substantial interest," the Warren
opinion stated. Five members of the Court accepted Warren's view
that the Walker judgment should be reversed because there was no
knowing or reckless falsehood.[39] The four remaining justices accepted Harlan's view that there was no "highly unreasonable
conduct" departing from accepted publishing standards in rapid
dissimination of the Associated Press dispatch.[40] The correspondent, the Harlan opinion stated, was present at the scene and gave
every indication of being competent.

The *Butts* case was not so simple, though his $460,000 judgment
was upheld by the Court. The alignment of justices, again, was 5–4,
but it was different than the alignment as to the proper standard for
use in "public-figure" cases. The four justices subscribing to the
Harlan opinion upheld the judgment by saying the *Saturday Evening Post*'s conduct was highly unreasonable and constituted "an
extreme departure from the standards of investigation and reporting ordinarily adhersed to by responsible publishers."[41] They also
said punitive damages, which Butts had received, were not prevented by the Constitution. They were joined by Justice Warren
alone among the other justices. Warren said the evidence showed
that the *Post* had been reckless in disregarding the truth.[42]

Warren cited the "slipshod and sketchy" investigatory techniques
employed by the *Saturday Evening Post* but grounded his decision
on the fact that the magazine "proceeding on its reckless course"
after being informed by Butts and his daughter that the article was

untrue.[43] There was full knowledge, he said, of the harm that likely would result from the publication. This was shown by the statements in the article that "Wally Butts will never help any football team again" and "careers will be ruined, that is sure."[44]

Even the Harlan opinion agreed that the lack of further investigation after being warned the article was false could arguably suffice to satisfy the "actual malice" standard.[45] But the four subscribing to this opinion based their decision on the lack of elementary investigation even though there was no pressure to publish. "Hot news" was not involved, and the information came from a questionable character—on probation—whose telephone call was unverified. Burnett's notes had never been seen by a *Post* employee and the football game had not been scrutinized. This was termed "highly unreasonable conduct."

Butts, then, won his award because four justices felt a jury could conclude there was an extreme departure from ordinary standards *and* because Chief Justice Warren felt the jury could find reckless disregard of the truth. Warren stood in the middle of an otherwise equally divided Court. While the other four justices could not agree that they should declare the *Saturday Evening Post* article libelous, they did join the chief justice in stating the *New York Times* rule applied to public figures as well as public officials. Justice William J. Brennan, Jr., and Justice Byron R. White felt that evidence showed reckless disregard of the truth. They said, however, that jurors had not been instructed in the standard.[46] Hence they were of the opinion that there should be a new trial.[47] Justices Hugo Black and William O. Douglas subscribed to the *New York Times* rule so there could be a majority view but stressed there should be no libel judgments under the First Amendment mandate.[48]

Justices Black and Douglas also warned against the Court's looking at facts in cases as though it were a jury. "What we do in these circumstances," Black's opinion stated, "is review the factual questions in cases decided by juries—a review which is a flat violation of the Seventh Amendment.[49] But the majority of the Court adhered to the principle that evidence could be reviewed to determine if jury judgments were consistent with "fundamental constitutional principles."[50]

Summary

Perhaps the jury system remained the greatest hope of public figures—and public officials—in obtaining libel judgments. Despite the Supreme Court's expressed authority to review libel cases anew, such a review was to determine *only* if constitutional principles were properly applied to the facts. So long, then, as lower court judges properly charged juries and evidence in a trial could support a finding of actual malice—the knowing or reckless falsehood—it would appear that the Supreme Court would have to declare a jury verdict proper.[51] Further, juries, in measuring publishers' conduct or knowledge, could render widely differing verdicts. This could not be standardized by the new constitutional rule of privilege.

Considerable effort had been made by the Court, however, to standardize the term *public figure*. Both Butts and Walker had been prominent in their own right, and Butts had been declared a public figure entirely because of his position as a university athletic director. Walker, on the other hand, had been declared a public figure because he injected himself into the center of an important public controversy. They obviously fit the general guidelines given by Chief Justice Warren to the effect that public figures were individuals, possibly from groups, who by fame, position, or involvement were influential in shaping issues of concern to the public. And these guidelines appeared to be quite adequate for lower federal and state courts to immediately and widely require such individuals to prove actual malice in seeking libel damages.[52]

As was shown by the *Butts* case, however, actual malice could be proved. Though part of the court felt the *Saturday Evening Post* had incurred responsibility for libeling a public figure by highly unreasonable conduct, Butts could not have obtained his judgment unless at least one justice—Chief Justice Warren—felt the magazine had published with actual malice in recklessly disregarding the truth. And one clear standard was set. If a publisher proceeded to publish after being informed of falsity—apparently a more than normal awareness of falsity—reckless disregard of the truth could be implied if there was no follow-up investigation. As Chief Justice

Warren put it, knowledge of harm would have been signaled to the publisher.

Redress for malicious calumniation, then, was still available. The Supreme Court standard had made it extremely difficult for a public figure—or a public official—to obtain damages for defamatory falsehoods. But it had not made damages impossible.

This, in the area of libel, was the legacy of the Warren Court. In a period of big government and powerful interests, that Court had decided that society had a First Amendment right for freer discussion of dominating, influential, and prominent people who shaped public issues. That discussion could even include defamatory falsehoods about public officials and public figures that were not intentionally or recklessly told. The Court had greatly narrowed the area of libel while enlarging freedom of speech and the press.

6/ A Constitutional Command
Libel Rule Is Explained, Enforced

In the four-year period immediately following the *Curtis Publish-ing Co. v. Butts* decisions, the Supreme Court issued a series of opinions in which lower federal and state courts were "instructed" in the use of the new constitutional rule of libel. In issuing these opinions, the Court more sharply defined the standard of a "know-ing or reckless falsehood." And it also clarified some other points. For instance, the Court had occasion to reiterate that the constitu-tional standard—despite the many opinions in *Curtis Publishing Co.*—was the same for public figures and public officials, and that this category definitely included candidates for office. It also called attention to the fact that the constitutional standard had been "re-formulated" to protect discussion of *anything* in both officials' and candidates' private lives that affected fitness for office. Above all, though, the Court in this series of opinions put the lower federal and state courts on notice that the new libel standard it had enun-ciated was not optional.[1] It was a constitutional command, and that command would be enforced.

The first occasion for enforcement came when a West Virginia court awarded a court clerk a $5,000 libel verdict for editorials written about the clerk's conduct during his reelection campaign. The jury in making the award had been allowed to consider "bad or corrupt motives" or "personal spite, ill will or a desire to injure plaintiff."[2] This fell woefully short of the requirement that false criticism had to be published with knowledge of falsity or reckless disregard of truth. Hence the Supreme Court granted certorari, in effect a demand that records of the trial be sent to it for review. Then, in a per curiam opinion issued 12 June 1967, the Court made it clear that West Virginia courts could not award damages for false editorial comment—even if with ill will—without convincingly clear proof that there was a "high degree of awareness of probable falsity" when it was written.[3]

This opinion, *Beckley Newspapers Corp.* v. *Hanks,* concerned a case that had actually been tried in state courts after the new public-official rule of libel had been declared. As the Supreme Court put it: "Although this action was tried subsequent to the decisions of the Court in New York Times v. Sullivan . . . Garrison v Louisiana . . . and Rosenblatt v. Baer . . . and despite the fact that it was recognized at the trial that the principles of *New York Times* were applicable, this case went to the jury on instructions which were clearly impermissible."[4] The Court had previously said in the *Garrison* case that a publisher's ill will or actual desire to injure an official could not be grounds for awarding a libel judgment.

There is no doubt that the editorials, in the *Beckley Post-Herald,* were designed to injure reelection chances of the official, C. Harold Hanks. One had said Hanks and a woman official stood alone on a controversial issue, told of threats he had made to newsmen, and said that "perhaps his blustering threats were able to intimidate the lady." At the trial, both the woman official and Hanks denied she had been threatened, and the jury found the newspaper statements stemmed entirely from supposition. The president of the newspaper had testified that "it was our opinion that that was as near the facts and truth as we could get," but that no investigation had been made before the editorial was written.

The Supreme Court said failure to make a prior investigation did not even constitute proof sufficient to present the question of a knowing or reckless falsehood to the jury.[5] It said: "Our examination of the whole record satisfies us that the proof presented to show actual malice lacks the convincing clarity which the constitutional standard demands."[6] The judgment was reversed. In its review, the Court had made it clear that the constitutional standard was a "demand" that state courts had to follow. Evidence of a knowing or reckless falsehood had to be with "convincing clarity," and jury instructions short of this standard were "impermissible." The message was that the judge should have issued a summary judgment as there was not a jury issue of a knowing or reckless falsehood.

This, perhaps, pinpointed the haziness of the "knowing or reckless falsehood" standard. And the Supreme Court tried to shed some light on the dimensions of the standard in the case of *St. Amant* v. *Thompson,* decided in April 1968. In this decision, the Court recognized that there could be no single infallible definition for the term "reckless falsehood," that "inevitably its outer limits will be worked out by case-to-case adjudication."[7] By using the word adjudication, the Court left no doubt that judges, and more specifically the justices of the Supreme Court, would determine what reckless falsehood meant. Working within the definition, the Court said, the burden then rested with juries to determine if and when knowing or reckless falsehoods had been published. As was stated in the opinion, the finders of fact "must determine whether the publication was indeed made in good faith."[8]

The good faith of Phil A. St. Amant, a candidate for the United States Senate in opposition to Sen. Russell B. Long, was at issue in this case. By the time the Supreme Court rendered its decision, the case already had a long and varied history in Louisiana courts. It orginally was filed in 1962 by the sheriff's deputy Herman A. Thompson after St. Amant, in a television equal-time broadcast, criticized labor union activity in Louisiana politics. In doing so, he repeated a labor union official's sworn affidavit accusing the president of a Teamsters Union local of passing money to Deputy Thompson. From this, St. Amant continued to say there was no way to tell how much influence the union president had with the sheriff's office.

Thompson, who was not connected with the political campaign, won a $5,000 verdict for libel. St. Amant appealed, and meanwhile the United States Supreme Court rendered the *New York Times* v. *Sullivan* decision. The Louisiana Court of Appeals held, as a result, that Thompson as a deputy sheriff was a public official who had to prove that a knowing or reckless falsehood had been broadcast. The court said that he had not, and the decision was reversed.[9] The appeals court also followed the Supreme Court's *Farmer's Cooperative* v. *WDAY, Inc.,* decision and held that the television station could not be held responsible under the equal-time provision of the Federal Communication Commission regulations. However, the Louisiana Supreme Court reversed the appeals court decision, other than the television ruling. It stated the trial evidence did show the broadcast was made with reckless disregard of the truth and that the trial court judgment was not inconsistent with constitutional guarantees.[10] The case then went to the United States Supreme Court.

The nation's highest court held in an 8–1 decision that St. Amant's broadcast could not be held libelous.[11] It was admitted that he falsely charged a sheriff's deputy with a crime by relying only on the sworn word of a union official without trying to verify the change. But the Court, in an opinion written by Justice Byron R. White, said that the standard of actual malice could not be measured "on what a reasonably prudent man" would publish or would investigate before publishing.[12] The Court stated: "There must be sufficient evidence to permit the conclusion that the defendant in fact entertained serious doubts as to the truth of his publication. Publishing with such doubts shows reckless disregard for truth or falsity and demonstrates actual malice."[13] There was no evidence that St. Amant seriously doubted the truth of his broadcast statements. Hence the Court reversed the decision, saying the Supreme Court of Louisiana had misunderstood the actual malice standard.

The Supreme Court pointed out that its previous cases had furnished "meaningful guidance for the further definition of a reckless publication."[14] Citing the *New York Times* case, the Court said Montgomery Commissioner Sullivan had failed to prove that the newspaper was *aware* that it was circulating false information.[15] Further, the Court said in *Garrison* v. *Louisiana* it had been held that there had to be a "high degree of awareness . . . of probable falsity" before a judgment could be rendered. And Justice Harlan's opinion in *Curtis Publishing Co.* v. *Butts* was quoted to the effect that "evidence of either deliberate falsehood or reckless publication despite the publisher's awareness of probable falsity was essential to recovery by a public officer."[16] These were the boundaries of actual malice as defined by the Court.

Within these definitions, the Court also provided limited guidelines for jurors in finding when the knowing or reckless falsehood standard had been abused. Specifically, the Court said: "Professions of good faith will be unlikely to prove persuasive, for example, where a story is fabricated by the defendant, is the product of his imagination, or is based wholly on an unverified anonymous telephone call. Nor will they be likely to prevail when the publisher's allegations are so inherently improbable that only a reckless man would have put them in circulation. Likewise recklessness may be found where there are obvious reasons to doubt the veracity of the informant or the accuracy of his reports."[17] These observations were not necessary for the Supreme Court to determine the case at issue. They were needed only to clarify the changing law as it pertained to libeling public officials.

The clarification indicated that jurors had considerable more leeway than judges. Judges in effect were commanded to charge juries that falsehood had to be deliberate or published recklessly despite an awareness of probable falsity. Jurors were provided instances under which they could determine abuse, but it was evident from the decision that determinations were not meant to be confined to these instances. Guidelines, not boundary lines, had been given for jury findings.

Notice also had been given that the findings of juries, as well as the rulings of judges, were subject to review by the Supreme Court to assure that the constitutional right of discussion would not be abridged. Such reviews, however, were not automatic or even desirable if proper procedural and substantive protections were taken at the lower court level. In fact, over the next two years the Supreme Court denied reviews in three cases in which the actual malice standard had been weighed by judges or juries.[18] In one of these cases, a libel award had been granted to a public official. By refusing to grant certiorari in the case, the Court provided undisputable evidence that it would not disturb a proper verdict for an official.

The particular official was 1964 Republican presidential candidate Barry Goldwater, who sued *Fact* magazine and its publisher, Ralph Ginzburg. His action followed a special issue of the magazine, "The Unconscious of a Conservative," which had been published during the 1964 campaign. The thrust of two major articles in the magazine was that Goldwater was mentally unbalanced, a dangerous lunatic, and unfit to be president. He sued for $1 million and was awarded $75,001. The trial jury in federal court found that the magazine had been printed with reckless disregard for the truth and that Ginzburg had deliberately assassinated the character of Goldwater by printing falsehoods.[19]

One *Fact* article purportedly was based on psychiatrists' replies to 12,356 questionnaires, which claimed that Goldwater had suffered a mental breakdown. At the trial both Goldwater and his family physician testified he had never suffered a mental break-down, and the pollster B. W. Roper testified the facts in the questionnaire were "loaded" and "slanted."[20] Further, before Ginzburg published the article, he was notified by the director of the American Psychiatric Association that his survey was invalid because responses were sought from psychiatrists who had not made personal examinations. Ginzburg was, in effect, made aware of the probable falsity of the poll results before publication. Additionally the trial record showed that only selected portions of the replies were printed. These out-of-context passages were frequently altered, abridged, and combined with other statements from other replies. All replies favorable to Goldwater were omitted from the article. It is no wonder, then, that the jury found Ginzburg deliberately set out to libel Goldwater.[21]

The jury verdict went undisturbed when the United States Supreme Court in 1970 denied certiorari to review.[22] However, Justice Hugo L. Black, joined by Justice William O. Douglas, dissented, stating the judgment against Ginzburg was "repressive" and "ominous." Black's dissent stated: "The public has an unqualified right to have the character and fitness of anyone who aspires to the presidency held up for the closest scrutiny. Extravagant, reckless statements and even claims which may not be true seem to be inevitable and perhaps essential part of the process by which voting public informs itself of the qualities of a man who would be president."[23] The dissenting justices also took a verbal slap at the punitive damages awarded in the case. Only $1 was to compensate Goldwater for harm to his reputation; $75,000 had been for punitive damages. Black's opinion said this punishment for exercising privileges of speech in public affairs was "incomprehensible."

Such a word—incomprehensible—might well have served to describe the views of all Supreme Court justices concerning a $17,500 libel judgment it reviewed in 1970. The judgment had been granted to Charles S. Bresler, a prominent real estate developer in Greenbelt, Maryland, because the local newspaper, *Greenbelt News Review*, had published derogatory remarks made about him in two city council meetings. His negotiating position with the council had been termed "blackmail" by some in attendance at the meetings because he demanded rezoning of his property before selling other property to the city for a school. The newspaper had accurately reported the heated public debate, but he sued, claiming the blackmail charge was printed even though those at the newspaper *knew* he was not guilty of the crime of blackmail.

The Supreme Court granted certiorari to review the decision and in May 1970, in the case of *Greenbelt Cooperative Publishing Association* v. *Bresler,* issued a unanimous opinion overturning his libel award. The Court said the jury award, made on the basis of either reckless disregard *or* "spite, hostility or deliberate intention to harm," was an "error of constitutional magnitude." Bresler, the Court said, was a public figure and could not obtain a judgment unless he proved specifically that there was knowledge of falsity or reckless disregard of falsity.[24] It said: "Debate on public issues will not be uninhibited if the speaker must run the risk that it will be proved in court that he spoke out of hatred. . . . And the constitutional prohibition in this respect is no different whether the plaintiff be considered a 'public official' or a 'public figure.' "[25] This was the first occasion for the Court, since its unusual split in the *Curtis Publishing Co.* v. *Butts* case, to clearly enunciate that the same libel rule applied to public figures that applied to public officials. Moreover, the *Bresler* opinion was written by Justice Potter Stewart, who in the *Butts* decision had not wanted to adopt the public-official rule for public figures. And the *Bresler* decision was unanimous.

The decision, though, did not stop by saying instructions to the jury were improper. In an independent review of the record, the Court said the subject of the suit—newspaper reports of public meetings of citizens discussing government affairs—"is one of particular First Amendment concern." The Court said: "The Greenbelt News Review was performing its wholly legitimate function as a community newspaper when it published full reports of the public debates in its news columns. If the reports had been truncated or distorted in such a way as to extract the word 'blackmail' from the context in which it was used at the public meeting, this would be a different case. But the report was accurate and full."[26] The report had given all positions in the public debate, and the Court said no reader could have thought the word "blackmail" charged a criminal offense. The word was no more than "rhetorical hyperbole, a vigorous epithet," and the Court said: "We hold that the imposition of liability on such a basis was constitutionally impermissible—that as a matter of constitutional law, the word "blackmail" in these circumstances was not slander when spoken, and not libel when reported in the Greenbelt News Review."[27] In this way the Court dismissed the contention that the newspaper printed criminal charges of "blackmail" while *knowing* it was not true. The Court said the newspaper did not depart from even ordinary publishing standards, let alone publish a knowing or reckless falsehood.[28]

Judicial instructions in lower courts concerning the knowing and reckless falsehood test, then, were being closely scrutinized by the Supreme Court. The Court was using the writ of certiorari to make sure that judges properly followed the law. And within a year after the *Bresler* decision, petitions for certiorari were granted by the Court to review three other questionable decisions.

In one of these decisions, a judge had allowed a jury to determine that "purely private libel" was involved in publishing a candidate's alleged criminal record of twenty-six years before. Hence the calculated-reckless falsehood standard was not followed. In another case, a jury had been instructed that a libel accusing an official of the crime of perjury, unrelated to his office, concerned only his private life and hence did not fall under constitutional protections. In the third case, a court instructed that a jury trial be held to determine whether a knowing or reckless falsehood was involved in a claimed inaccurate and unfair report of a government document, the result of which made allegations against a police officer appear to be established fact. The Supreme Court disagreed with all these judicial orders, and they were overturned in separate but companion opinions written by Justice Potter Stewart and issued on 24 February 1971.

The first of these cases, *Monitor Patriot Co. v. Roy,* was filed after the syndicated columnist Drew Pearson wrote a "Washington Merry-Go-Round" column about New Hampshire's Democratic party primary election.[29] The column, carried in the *Concord Daily Monitor* and the *New Hampshire Patriot,* listed the criminal records of several candidates and described Alphonse Roy, one of the candidates, as a "former small-time bootlegger." Roy sued for libel, and evidence was presented at the trial that Roy had been a bootlegger during the Prohibition era. The judge instructed that the jury should determine if private or public libel was involved. And the jury awarded Roy $20,000 in damages after finding that the charge, based on alleged activities twenty-six years before, was "purely private libel" outside the protection of the constitutional actual malice rule.

The instructions had been given in an attempt to let jurors find if "official conduct" was involved. The judge had ruled that a candidate must make the same proofs as an official if this was the case. Official conduct, the judge had instructed, would include "so much of his private character as affects his fitness for office." However, he also said if the bootlegging charge would not touch on fitness but was "rather a bringing forward of the plaintiff's long forgotten misconduct in which the public had no interest, then it would be a private matter in the private sector."[30] Additionally he instructed that if the jury found the publication to be in the "private sector," justification would require a finding that the article was true and published on a "lawful occasion."

In returning a verdict for Roy, as the Supreme Court of the United States said on review, it was possible that the jury had found the charge true but not published on a "lawful occasion."[31] This "syllogistic manipulation of distinctions between the 'private sectors' and the 'public sectors' and matters of fact and matters of law" was termed by the Court to be of little use in resolving First Amendment protections. And while the Court said it might be preferable to term a candidate for office a "public figure" as opposed to a "public official," the distinction was not important because: "Whichever term is applied, publications concerning candidates must be accorded at least as much protection under the First Amendment as those concerning occupants of public office."[32] The jury, it said, had far too much leeway in determining if the statement charging bootlegging activities twenty-six years previously was "private libel" and not relevant to fitness and hence not within First Amendment protections.[33]

In discussing "relevancy," the Court pointed out that the *New York Times* "official conduct" standard had been *reformulated* in *Garrison* v. *Louisiana* to include "anything which might touch on an official's fitness for office."[34] This, the Court said, applied with "special force to the case of a candidate." As the unanimous Court put it: "The candidate who vaunts his spotless record and sterling integrity cannot convincingly cry 'Foul!' when an opponent or an industrious reporter attempts to demonstrate the contrary."[35] Further, the Court said it could not permit "liability for political speech which 'more probably than otherwise' in the opinion of the jury 'would not touch upon or be relevant' to a candidate's fitness for office."[36] A *relevancy* test, the Court said, could become an instrument of suppression.[37]

Hence, the Court said, the judgment of the lower court had to be reversed. The crux of the opinion stated: "We therefore hold as a matter of constitutional law that a charge of criminal conduct, no matter how remote in time or place, can never be irrelevant to an official's or a candidate's fitness for office for purposes of application of the knowing or reckless disregard rule of *New York Times* v. *Sullivan*."[38] Specifically, then, discussion of candidates carried the same constitutional protection as discussion of officials. And the Court said that while the mental element of "knowing and reckless disregard" is not always easy of ascertainment,[39] this standard had to be followed even with charges of crime against a candidate.

With the exception that a public official was involved, the identical conclusion was reached by a united Supreme Court in *Ocala Star-Banner Co.* v. *Damron,* issued on the same day.[40] This case arose when the *Ocala Star-Banner,* a Florida newspaper serving several counties, falsely accused a garage owner, Leonard Damron, of having been indicted in federal court for perjury. Damron also was mayor of Crystal City, one of the communities the newspaper served, and also was a candidate for county tax assessor. But this was not mentioned in the story. As a matter of fact, Damron's brother James had been indicted, and the Crystal City correspondent had written the story correctly. However, a new area editor on the newspaper had handled several stories about Leonard Damron, had never heard of his brother, had concluded the correspondent made an error, and had changed the name before publication. The result was a charge of crime against an innocent man and a suit for libel.

During the trial, the Florida judge instructed jurors that the "knowing or reckless falsehood" standard was not applicable because the newspaper publication made no reference to the public offices held by Damron. Damron's private life and not official conduct, he said, was the basis of the falsehood.[41] However, on review, the United States Supreme Court cited the *Monitor Patriot Co.* case and said that official conduct did not have to be involved. It said: "Under any test we can conceive, the charge that a local mayor and candidate for a county elective post has been indicted for perjury in a civil rights suit is relevant to his fitness for office."[42] The trial court judgment was reversed. The Supreme Court said there could be no judgment unless it was proved with convincing clarity that the newspaper publication was made with knowledge of falsity or reckless disregard of falsity. Again, the Court had overturned a case because of improper instructions to a jury.

And the Court said there wasn't even a jury issue in the last of the three cases, *Time, Inc., v. Pape*.[43] This case involved a *Time* magazine review of an official 307-page report entitled *Justice*, issued by the United States Commission on Civil Rights. The magazine reviewed parts of the document purportedly dealing with what the commission called "typical cases of police brutality" that deserved discussion.[44] The report stated the cases were based on allegations not conclusively determined but supported by either convictions, impartial findings, sworn testimony, affidavits, or staff investigations. But it listed the allegations under headings such as "Unlawful Police Violence" and used them to conclude that police brutality was a serious, continuing problem that needed to be corrected.[45] *Time*, in its review, summarized one of the listed cases involving a Chicago detective, Frank Pape, without indicating the charges were alleged or were not independent findings of the Commission.[46] Pape sued in federal court.

Time was granted a summary judgment at the trial on the basis that there was no jury issue of a knowing or reckless falsehood. But a U.S. court of appeals ordered a trial to determine if by departing from the fidelity of the official report the magazine acted with reckless disregard of the truth.[47] The Supreme Court granted certiorari, overturned the jury trial order and sustained the summary judgment.

In an 8–1 decision, the Supreme Court said the commission's report was ambiguous and that words used in different parts of the document could indicate the commission believed the complaints were valid.[48] As the Court said: "*Time*'s omission of the word 'alleged' amounted to the adoption of one of a number of possible rational interpretations of a document that bristled with ambiguities. The deliberate choice of such an interpretation, though arguably reflecting a misconception, was not enough to create a jury issue of 'malice' under *New York Times.*"[49] The Court further said that "misinterpretation of the gist of a lengthy government document" is not reckless disregard of the truth.[50]

Both the *Time* author and editorial researcher had testified in district court that the word "alleged" was omitted because the context of the full *Justice* report showed to them that the commission believed the Pape incident had occurred.[51] The Supreme Court said at most this reflected "an error of judgment."[52] However, the Court issued a warning in the opinion that the word "alleged" still was needed in published reports of information damaging to reputation. The decision was limited to a news report of an ambiguous government publication that had equated allegations with *specific grounds* for a "serious problem in the United States."[53] This was not, as the Court said, a "conventional libel case."[54]

Summary

Six libel cases had been reviewed by the Supreme Court in four years, and judges' orders and instructions to jurors had been over-turned in each as falling short of constitutional requirements. The Court had made it clear that it would tolerate nothing short of proving the "mental element" necessary for showing the knowing or reckless falsehood in cases dealing with public officials, public figures, and candidates for office. Further, the Court underscored the reformulation of this standard to include discussion about officials' and candidates' private actions affecting their public life. This included accusations of crime, though they may have occurred long ago and though they were unrelated to office or campaign. Anything relevant to fitness fell under protected discussion, and jurors could not be allowed to determine that such discussion fell in a so-called private sector so far as libel was concerned. Neither could they bring in judgments based on "ill will," "bad motives," or publications designed "to injure" public men.

Yet the Court had shown, by refusing to review the *Goldwater* case, that it would not disturb a proper libel verdict for a candidate or official, even when punitive damages were awarded. In this case, the publisher had been made aware that the basis of his articles—the results of his slanted survey—was probably false. Still he continued to change and eliminate the results to publish the story he wanted. This fell within the definition of a "knowing or reckless falsehood" issued by the Court—that falsehoods had to be deliberate or published recklessly despite a high degree of awareness of probable falsity. The same standard applied, the Court said, concerning reports of heated public debate in citizen meetings to discuss government affairs.

The Court even found an opportunity to instruct jurors as to when they might find publications went beyond constitutional protection. This might occur when stories were fabricated, the product of imagination, or based on unverified telephone calls. It also could occur when articles were published despite obvious reasons to doubt the truthfulness of the sources or when stories were so improbable that only a reckless man would publish them. But lack of prior investigation or errors of interpretation could not be considered as jury issues in determining actual malice. In effect, summary judgments were endorsed when proofs of the knowing or reckless falsehood were lacking. And the Court made it clear that the knowing and reckless falsehood standard was not based on what a reasonably prudent man would publish.

In these six cases, the Court had restated, reinterpreted, and explained the constitutional law of libel. It was obviously recognized that the law was defined but not refined. Clarification came with each decision. But the basics were continually stressed to assure that the law was applied uniformly in lower courts across the nation. The Court had even given a practical demonstration that the law applied uniformly to media. In the *St. Amant* case, which originated on television, the privilege for anyone to discuss public officials had been shown as a fair equivalent of the preferred privilege of discussion previously granted to the electronic media through Federal Communications Commission regulations. The *St. Amant* case was the last libel decision in which Chief Justice Earl Warren participated. But there appeared to be no change in the Court's direction under the new chief justice, Warren Burger. Constitutional protections for free discussion had even become more pronounced in *Greenbelt, Monitor Patriot Co., Ocala Star-Banner,* and *Time,*

Inc., v. *Pape*. The case-by-case adjudication had given explicit recognition to the continual development of the law of libel. But the so-called outer limits of this law—in reality a constitutional command—had not yet been reached.

7/ A Constitutional Dilemma
Court Splits on Privilege to Discuss Issues

When the Supreme Court on 7 June 1971 issued a many faceted decision in the case of *Rosenbloom* v. *Metromedia, Inc.*, it appeared that the constitutional privilege in libel cases could have reached its so-called outer limits. The Court in this case upheld a lower federal court in requiring that a knowing or reckless falsehood be proved before libel damages could be obtained by a private individual who claimed he was defamed in broadcasts discussing a police campaign to enforce obscenity laws.[1] The surface conclusion was that the Supreme Court had extended the constitutional privilege of discussion—previously limited to public officials and public figures—to include libels of private individuals that occurred in discussion of public issues. And it had—to an extent. But the impetus for the decision had come in a plurality, not a majority, opinion. And it was only partially endorsed in separate opinions by two concurring justices, one of whom stipulated that public issues being discussed had to focus on public officials.

Actually, the Court was badly fractured in this decision. Five separate opinions were written, and there were just as many justices dissenting—three—as there were signing the plurality holding. However, all eight of the justices taking part in the decision did have one view in common. All said in their opinions that the Constitution protects, to some extent or another, published falsehoods concerning private individuals. While the dissenters would not adopt the knowing or reckless falsehood standard as applied to discussion of public issues, they did say the First Amendment protected nonnegligent falsehoods about private individuals in all libel cases, whether or not public issues were being discussed. And they would have greatly reduced the authority of the states to award

72

compensatory and punitive damages. Hence the opinions of all justices would have afforded more protection to the media in private libel suits than there had been in the past.

The best interpretation of the *Rosenbloom* v. *Metromedia, Inc.,* decision, as such, was given in the separate opinion of Justice Byron R. White. Pointing out that Justices Hugo Black and William O. Douglas would support any view restricting libel, since they believed the Constitution prevented all libel actions, White stated both the plurality and dissenting views had the support of five justices. Hence the Court, White said, would support each of the following rules: "For public officers and public figures to recover for damages to their reputations for libelous falsehoods, they must prove either knowing or reckless disregard of the truth. All other plaintiffs must prove at least negligent falsehood, but if the publication about them was in an area of legitimate public interest, then they too must prove deliberate or reckless error. In all actions for libel or slander, actual damages must be proved, and awards of punitive damages will be strictly limited."[2] The decision as it stood truly revolutionized the private law of libel.

While the decision was rendered in mid-1971, the events that triggered it had occured in late 1963. George Rosenbloom, a distributor of nudist magazines in Philadelphia, was arrested along with about twenty newsstand operators on charges of selling obscene materials. Police raided his home and warehouse and seized his magazines. At the time, the police captain informed the media. All news outlets reported the events, and radio station WIP, owned by Metromedia, Inc., broadcast the news of the arrest eight times at half-hour intervals. In each, the radio station said police had arrested "smut merchants," and in the first two broadcasts had said three thousand obscene books had been confiscated from Rosenbloom. Later broadcasts had called the books "reportedly obscene."[3]

When Rosenbloom went to court to seek an injunction to prohibit further police interference with his business, the result was ten additional WIP broadcasts. In these it was said the injunction was to force officials "to lay off the smut literature racket." It also referred to the distributor, though Rosenbloom was not mentioned by name, as a "girlie-book peddler," and said the city's effort in arrests was to "rid the city of pornography." After these broadcasts, Rosenbloom went to station WIP and talked to a newscaster over a lobby telephone, saying he had a public statement from the district attorney that declared the magazines were completely legal. The newsman then "hung up" the telephone and terminated the conversation. After this, the only other story broadcast by WIP was checked with the judge before broadcast. It still said the district attorney claimed the publications were "smut" and "immoral literature."

When Rosenbloom was acquitted of obscenity charges some six months later, with a ruling that the nudist magazines were not obscene, he filed a libel suit in federal district court against Metromedia's station, WIP. He said WIP called the books obscene, and that this was proved false by his acquittal. He also claimed statements were false in the broadcasts characterizing him as a "smut distributor," a "girlie-book peddler" and a participant in "the smut literature racket."[4] At the trial, jurors found that WIP had forfeited its privilege to fairly and accurately report even false statements by officials—either by intent to injure Rosenbloom or by "want of reasonable care . . . to ascertain the truth."[5] Rosenbloom won a verdict of $25,000 in general damages and $750,000 in punitive damages. The judge reduced the punitive damages to $250,000.

This trial verdict was reversed by the Court of Appeals for the Third Circuit. That court ruled the broadcasts concerned a matter of public interest and hence the *New York Times* standard applied. Rosenbloom's proofs, it said, did not meet that standard. The fact that Rosenbloom was not a public figure was not accorded "decisive significance" because it was ruled that the First Amendment protected public issue discussion. It was this ruling that the Supreme Court of the United States upheld in *Rosenbloom* v. *Metromedia, Inc.*

The Supreme Court's judgment, though fragmented, was led by the plurality opinion, written by Justice William J. Brennan, Jr., and subscribed to by Chief Justice Warren Burger and Justice Harry Blackmun. The opinion stated:

It is clear that there has emerged from our cases decided since the *New York Times* the concept that the First Amendment's impact upon state libel laws derives not so much from whether the plaintiff is a "public official," "public figure," or "private individual," as it derives from the question

whether the allegedly defamatory publication concerns a matter of public
or general interest. . . . In that circumstance we think the time has come
forthrightly to announce that the determinant whether the First Amendment applies to state libel actions is whether the utterance involved concerns an issue of public or general concern, albeit leaving the delineation of
the reach of that term to future cases.[6]

The holding of this opinion was that *all people*—whether anonymous individuals, public officials, or public figures—had to give
clear and convincing proof of calculated or reckless falsehoods before they could collect damages for defamation published or broadcast about public issues. And public issues were defined by the
plurality as being matters of public or general concern.[7]

The rationale of the plurality was simply that an artificial barrier
had been built up in previous libel decisions between "public and
private" people so far as the public's interest was concerned.[8] This
view was expressed as follows: "If a matter is a subject of public or
general interest, it cannot suddenly become less so merely because a
private individual is involved, or because in some sense the individual did not 'voluntarily' choose to become involved. The public's
primary interest is in the event; the public focus is on the conduct of
the participant and the content, effect and significance of the conduct, not the participant's prior anonymity or notoriety."[9] The
Rosenbloom case illustrated the point, the opinion stated. Here
citizens had a vital interest in seeing that obscenity laws were enforced while also seeing that free expression was not suppressed.
Whether the magazine distributor was famous or a private busi-
nessman, the assertion was that it had no relevance to the interest in
the issue. Police arrest of anyone for distributing allegedly obscene
magazines, it was stated, "clearly constitutes an issue of public or
general interest."[10]

If the media did not have a constitutional privilege of libel to
discuss individuals involved in public issues, as it did for public
figures, the opinion said a "dampening" of discussion would result.[11] Whether individuals thrust themselves into issues or not was
given little importance as "voluntarily or not, we are all 'public
men' to some degree."[12] The opinion said it was a *legal fiction* that
public figures voluntarily expose their lives to public inspection,
while private individuals keep theirs shrouded from public view.[13]

It also discounted the argument that private individuals do not have access to the media to counter defamatory matter that corresponds to that enjoyed by public men. It was claimed that the media's continued interest in an issue determines the ability of anyone— private individual, public figure, or public official—to respond through the media.

Turning to the case itself, the plurality pointed to the fact that Rosenbloom's judgment came on a "preponderance of the evidence" and that the verdict was based on lack of reasonable care. Both were rejected as not providing adequate "breathing space" for freedom of speech and press.[14] None of the proofs showed convincing clarity of a calculated or reckless falsehood that the First Amendment required, according to the opinion. The strongest evidence was said to be when the WIP newscaster hung up the telephone without learning Rosenbloom's side of the case. But the opinion stated that "reckless conduct is not measured by whether a reasonably prudent man would have published, or would have investigated before publishing."[15] The only broadcast after the disrupted telephone conversation was confirmed by the judge involved, and the opinion stated there was no showing that there were serious doubts as to the truth of the report that the district attorney considered the magazine "smut" and "immoral literature."

This opinion drew concurrence from Justice Hugo L. Black, who agreed that the First Amendment protects "all discussion and communication involving matters of legitimate public concern, without regard to whether the persons involved are famous or anonymous." But while concurring in the judgment, he again expressed his view that the First Amendment did not allow any recovery in libel actions against the news media.[16] This undoubtedly would have been the opinion of Justice William O. Douglas, who refused to take part in the *Metromedia* case. He had been under fire for liberal opinions in obscenity cases, and obscenity, of course, was a peripheral issue in the case.

Justice White also concurred in the judgment, but not the plurality opinion, which he said displaced more state law than was necessary.[17] He said he would rest his decision on the *New York Times* case that gave broadcasting media and the press not only the right to censure and praise officials but "the concomitant right to censure and criticize their adversaries."[18] He would have held that the constitutional privilege to report on actions of public servants had "no requirement that the reputation or the privacy of an individual involved in or affected by the official action be spared from public view."[19] On this basis, he said, the WIP broadcast was privileged under the Constitution. "I would not, however, adjudicate cases not now before the Court," he wrote.[20]

In this regard, he said he was not convinced that the Court "must fashion a constitutional rule protecting a whole range of damaging falsehoods and so shift the burden from those who publish to those who are injured."[21] Here he was referring to both the plurality and the two dissenting opinions. None would have held publishers to the then prevailing strict liability rule in which they had to prove truth of statements published about private individuals.

The dissenters—Justices John Marshall Harlan, Thurgood Marshall, and Potter Stewart—all agreed that the Constitution prevents libel awards to private individuals on the basis of simple falsity. But they refused to go along with the "public issues" standard. This standard, they stated, was *not adequate to protect a free press or wrongful hurt to reputation.*[22] All events arguably were within the area of "public or general concern," they said, and hence the rule could not have general applicability.[23] Justice Marshall, joined by Justice Stewart, said the public issues standard would "require this Court to engage in a constant and continuing supervision of defamation litigation throughout the country."[24] And Justice Harlan in his opinion stated the plurality's standard would subject "the press to judicial second-guessing of the newsworthiness of each item they print."[25]

Hence each dissenting opinion endorsed a rule that they said was generally applicable and would provide adequate protection for both press freedom and reputation. This rule would be to restrict the award of damages to actual and measurable injuries.[26] As Justice Marshall wrote: "The unlimited discretion exercised by juries in awarding punitive and presumed damages compounds the problem of self-censorship that necessarily results from the awarding of huge judgments. This discretion allows juries to penalize heavily the unorthodox and the unpopular and exact little from others. Such freewheeling discretion presents obvious and basic threats to society's interest in freedom of the press."[27] Still, the two dissenting opinions differed somewhat on damage awards. Justices Marshall and Stewart would allow no punitive damages to be awarded and would limit all damages to actual injuries—including pecuniary losses and other losses related to some proven harm.[28] Justice Harlan would require that damages be limited to harms caused and then only to consequences of publication which could have been reasonably foreseen by publishers.[29] But Justice Harlan, unlike Justices Stewart and Marshall, also sanctioned punitive damages if private individuals also proved actual malice—the calculated or reckless falsehood.[30] Even then, though, he wrote that punitive damages had to bare "a reasonable and purposeful relationship to the actual harm done."[31]

The three justices obviously were concerned over the large $750,000 punitive damage award granted to Rosenbloom by the jury, and they would have sent the case back for retrial on their concepts of limited damages.[32] But they were not concerned with the basis—lack of reasonable care—under which the jury made the award. In fact, all the dissenters agreed that lack of reasonable care was a proper rule for constitutional privilege in discussing private individuals.

Their view was that the media should be exempt from libel damages unless private individuals could prove publishers were at fault in disseminating falsehoods.[33] Fault, they said, could be determined by negligence or lack of reasonable care.[34] However, both dissenting opinions pointed out that states could administer their own standards of fault.[35] Justice Harlan's view concerning his "reduced" privilege for discussing individuals, as opposed to public men, was as follows:

I do think there is a difference, relevant to the interests here involved between the public and private plaintiff, as our cases have defined these categories, and that maintaining a constitutional distinction between them is at least as likely to protect true First Amendment concerns as one that eradicates such a line and substitutes for it a distinction between matters we think are of true social significance and those we think are not.

To begin, it does no violence, in my judgment, to the value of freedom of speech and press to impose a duty of reasonable care upon those who would exercise these freedoms. I do not think it can be gainsaid that the States have a substantial interest in encouraging speakers to carefully seek the truth before they communicate, as well as in compensating persons actually harmed by false descriptions of their personal behavior.[36]

He also said he did not believe the nonpublic person should be held up to the same degree of scrutiny as public servants making official policy or public figures making nonofficial policy.[37] Nor did he believe the nonpublic person could gain access to the media to rebut falsehoods as easy as the public person. Hence, he said, the *New York Times* rule was inapplicable concerning private individuals.

While the dissenters, in Justice White's words, would "not roll back the state laws so far" as those subscribing to the plurality opinion,[38] all the justices would have changed the existing state laws. Nevertheless, because the view that the WIP broadcast was privileged under the Constitution was held by five justices, the plurality opinion carried the day. The decision's outward appearance was that the calculated or reckless falsehood had to be proved to collect damages on all libels resulting from discussion of matters of public concern. Further, judges in the lower courts of the nation almost immediately and uniformly accepted the plurality opinion as ruling law for libel cases they considered.

Summary

As had been predicted by the dissenters, almost everything published was considered by the lower courts as matters of "public or general concern" that required libel decisions to be based on the knowing or reckless falsehood standard. Within a year, for example, federal and state appellate courts applied the public-issue standard to stories about individuals involved in electronic eavesdropping, gun fights, organized crime, sports, backpacking overseas, pollution control, quality of restaurant food, service on private bus systems, suspension from school, selling liquor to minors, private divorce, published books, housing eviction, jail escapes, political campaign work, and credit bureau practices.[39] At least two courts ruled, however, that private credit reports—as opposed to bureau practices—were private matters that did not fall within the public issue sphere.[40] These cases, however, were exceptions.

The sweep of the assumed constitutional privilege to discuss public issues was so expansive that few libel cases were won by private individuals filing them. Logical arguments were made by those in the media that anything newsworthy had to be matters of public concern. And judges were responsive to the arguments. The momentum of the plurality ruling in *Rosenbloom* v. *Metromedia* had truly revolutionized the law of libel in the United States.

Even scholarly law journals at the time accepted the view that the constitutional protection had been changed from discussion of people to discussion of issues.[41] The view of the dissenters that private individuals must prove nonnegligent falsehoods in all libel cases—which could arguably be claimed to have as heavy weight in the decision itself as the plurality opinion—was basically ignored in the judicial rush to apply the more restrictive actual malice standard to most libel cases.[42]

It appeared, then, that the direction of the law had been plotted. But several directions had been taken in the *Metromedia* decision by the justices; they were badly split with no one view having more than three adherents. Additionally this was the last libel decision in which two of the justices—Black and Harlan—were to participate. Following their deaths, Justices Lewis F. Powell, Jr., and William H. Rehnquist were appointed to the Court by Pres. Richard M. Nixon. The fragile alignments in the *Metromedia* case at best were questionable. One could not say that the Supreme Court had stabilized the law of libel.

8/ Privilege to Discuss Individuals "Private Libel" Confined by *Gertz* v. *Welch*

In the three-year period following the Supreme Court decision in *Rosenbloom* v. *Metromedia,* some seventeen states and six United States courts of appeals followed the plurality opinion in that case as ruling law. Specifically, they held that there could be no libel judgment for "discussion and communication involving matters of public or general concern" without proof of a calculated or reckless falsehood.[1] One of these many holdings, in the Court of Appeals for the Seventh Circuit, came in the case of *Gertz* v. *Welch*. And this holding was reviewed by the Supreme Court, on a writ of certiorari, to "reconsider the extent of a publisher's constitutional privilege for defamation of a private citizen."[2]

Then, on 25 June 1974, a majority of the Supreme Court, mustered only because one justice felt a need to eliminate the "unsureness engendered by Rosenbloom's diversity," rejected the public issue rationale for libel cases.[3] Instead, the Court in a 5–4 opinion stated in effect that the "ordinary citizen, when libeled by a publication defamatory on its face, must prove some degree of culpability on the part of the publisher beyond the circulation to the public of a damaging falsehood."[4] It also held there had to be "competent evidence" of actual injury to reputation before any damages could be awarded.[5] Additionally there could be no presumed or punitive damages without proof that the publisher knew his communication was false or recklessly disregarded whether it was false or not. These standards were declared to be the "minimum" that states had to follow in awarding libel damages to private individuals.

For all practical purposes, the Court had adopted the view of the dissenters in the *Rosenbloom* case. The pendulum, in *Gertz* v. *Welch,* had swung in the opposite direction. With changes in the

Court itself, following the deaths of Justices Hugo L. Black and John Marshall Harlan, the new "perhaps evanescent majority," as one justice termed it,[6] was not prepared to accept the decision of the *Rosenbloom* plurality. All were agreed, however, that the constitutional privilege to discuss public men, short of the knowing or reckless falsehood, should not be disturbed.[7] And the new majority also agreed that the First Amendment demanded a privilege for some falsehood in publications concerning private individuals, "to protect speech that matters."[8] But the privilege for falsehood here was placed at a lower level than that for discussion of public men. The privilege concerning private individuals was limited only to the publication of no-fault or nonnegligent falsehoods.[9]

The publisher in this particular case was Robert Welch, founder of the John Birch Society and a long-time campaigner against communism. His magazine, *American Opinion,* carried an article in which the Chicago attorney Elmer Gertz claimed he was defamed. The article, written by a free-lance reporter and entitled "Frame Up: Richard Nuccio and the War on Police," told about the trial and conviction of the Chicago policeman Nuccio after he had shot and killed a Chicago youth. While Gertz had not been involved in the prosecution, he had been retained to represent the youth's family in civil action against Nuccio and had represented the family at the coroner's inquest. And the magazine article described him as a "Leninist" and a "Communist-fronter" who was an architect of the "frame-up" against Nuccio. The article also intimated Gertz had a criminal record and said he had been a member of the "Marxist League for Industrial Democracy."

This information contained serious inaccuracies, and the managing editor of *American Opinion* had made no effort to verify the charges. In fact, in publishing the article, the editor had included a picture of the attorney with the caption "Elmer Gertz of the Red Guild Harasses Nuccio." Gertz sued for libel. At the trial, Welch's defense was that Gertz was either a public figure or a public official and was involved in a public issue and hence was required to prove either a knowing or reckless falsehood to receive any damages. There was testimony to the effect that the editor had never heard of Gertz, relied entirely on the reporter, and had no serious doubt as to the truth of the publication. While the trial judge ruled that Gertz was neither a public figure nor public official, he reserved judgment on the public issue question. Following the trial, the jury brought in a $50,000 verdict for Gertz on the basis of strict liability. At this time the judge set aside the libel verdict on the basis that a public issue was involved and there was no proof of a knowing or reckless falsehood.[10]

Gertz appealed this decision, which came before the Supreme Court's ruling in the *Rosenbloom* case. However, the Court of Appeals for the Seventh Circuit considered the appeal shortly after the *Rosenbloom* decision. The appeals court questioned the district court's finding that Gertz was not a public figure. He had been active in community and professional affairs, had served on Chicago housing committees, had been an officer of local civic groups, and had published several books and articles on legal subjects.[11] Nevertheless, the court of appeals did not overturn the nonpublic-figure finding. Instead, it agreed with the district court, in light of *Rosenbloom,* that the public issue being discussed would require proof of a knowing and reckless falsehood, and that such proof had not been made by Gertz for a libel judgment.[12]

This was the decision reviewed by the Supreme Court. And the Court said the principal issue was whether a publisher of defamatory falsehoods about a *private individual* could claim a constitutional privilege against liability.[13] It was pointed out that consideration was given to such a privilege in the *Rosenbloom* case, but "no majority could agree on a controlling rationale."[14]

Here, in *Gertz* v. *Welch,* the Court said it was beginning with the common ground that "there is no such thing as a false idea."[15] The opinion stated that there was no libel in "error of opinion."[16] The Court said: "However pernicious an opinion may seem, we depend for its correction not on the conscience of judges or juries but on the competition of other ideas."[17] While differentiating between opinion and fact—an extremely important consideration for writers of editorials and commentary—the Court also recognized that false statements of *fact* were "inevitable in free debate." Hence the media could not, under the First Amendment, be held to strict liability and made to prove the truth of all injurious statements.[18]

But the question, the Court said, was how to balance the First Amendment requirement with the right of the states, under the Ninth and Tenth amendments, to protect private personality.[19] The constitutional rule for discussing public officials and public figures—liability for the knowing and reckless falsehood—was described as "correct" but a "substantial abridgement of the state law right to compensate for wrongful hurt to one's reputation."[20] Such an abridgement would not be appropriate in private-person libel cases, the Court said.

Its rationale, the exact opposite of the *Rosenbloom* plurality, was that private individuals are more deserving of recovery than public people because they do not seek public scrutiny and do not relinquish interest in the protection of their good names. Also, the Court said, states have more interest in protecting common people, as they do not have access to the media to combat defamatory falsehoods as do public people.[21] Hence the knowing and reckless falsehood test proposed by the *Rosenbloom* plurality "would abridge this legitimate state interest to a degree that we find unacceptable."[22]

In fashioning a standard to balance press freedom with the state's right to protect personal reputation, the Court said: "We hold that so long as they do not impose liability without fault, the States may define for themselves the appropriate standard of liability for a publisher or broadcaster of defamatory falsehood injurious to private individuals. . . . At least this conclusion obtains where, as here, the substance of the defamatory statement 'makes substantial danger to reputation apparent.' "[23] The Court stipulated that different considerations might be required if content of the article itself did not warn of the defamatory potential. Though no view on such considerations was expressed, the indication was that the actual malice standard—the knowing or reckless falsehood—might apply where libel was not apparent on the face of the publication.[24]

The majority opinion did not stop, however, in saying falsehoods had to be printed with fault before there could be a judgment. Holding that states had no interest in securing awards for those bringing libel suits in excess of actual injuries, the Court said:

It is therefore appropriate to require that state remedies for defamatory falsehood reach no further than is necessary to protect the legitimate interest involved. It is necessary to restrict defamation plaintiffs who do not prove knowledge of falsity or reckless disregard for the truth to compensation for actual injury. . . . Suffice it to say that actual injury is not limited to out-of-pocket loss. Indeed, the more customary types of actual harm inflicted by defamatory falsehood include impairment of reputation and standing in the community, personal humiliation, and mental anguish and suffering. Of course, juries must be limited by appropriate instructions, and all awards must be supported by competent evidence concerning the injury, although there need be no evidence which assigns an actual dollar value to the injury.[25]

Damages in all suits brought by private individuals, then, were limited to actual injury, based on *competent* evidence. No presumed or punitive damages would be allowed short of proving actual malice—the calculated or reckless falsehood. This restriction on damages, coupled with the minimum requirement that liability for false statements required a finding of fault, changed completely the nation's common law of libel.

Such a change, the majority felt, was required by the First Amendment. But it also required that the "public issue" protection granted by the *Rosenbloom* plurality be jettisoned. The Court again had adopted the rationale that the media was protected more when it discussed some people than when it discussed others. And in trying to differentiate between these people, the Court in the *Gertz* case said:

Hypothetically, it may be possible for someone to become a public figure through no purposeful action of his own, but the instances of truly involuntary public figures must be exceedingly rare. For the most part those who attain this status have assumed roles of especial prominence in the affairs of society. Some occupy positions of such persuasive power and influence that they are deemed public figures for all purposes. More commonly, those classed as public figures have thrust themselves into the forefront of particular controversies in order to influence the resolution of the issues involved. In either event, they invite attention and comment.

Even if the foregoing generalities do not obtain in every instance, the communications media are entitled to act on the assumption that public officials and public figures have voluntarily exposed themselves to increased risk of injury from defamatory falsehoods concerning them. No such assumption is justified with respect to a private individual.[26]

Interestingly, the opinion focused on those involved in "controversies," not those involved in what the *Curtis Publishing Co.* case called "matters of public concern."[27] And the indication was that the Court was backing away from the public-figure designation for those involuntarily *drawn* into controversies.

Evidence of this came when the Court looked at Gertz's participation in the public issue from which the defamation occurred. Here the justices said, in effect, that he had not injected himself nor was he drawn into a controversy to become a "public figure for a limited range of issues."[28] The reason given was that he had simply been representing a private client as a lawyer, had taken no part in the prosecution of the officer Nuccio, and had never discussed the civil suit against Nuccio with the press. Hence he had not thrust himself into a controversy, nor had he invited the public's attention to influence the outcome.[29] He had not drawn public attention until the *American Opinion* publication itself, which was the focus of the libel suit. And as an "officer of the court" by virtue of being an attorney, the Court said, he was not a public official.

Also, the Court said, Gertz had not achieved "such pervasive fame or notoriety that he becomes a public figure for all purposes and in all contexts."[30] The fact that he was long active in community and professional affairs, had been an officer of civic groups, had published several books and articles on legal subjects was discounted by the Court. None of the prospective jurors at his libel trial had ever heard of Gertz, the Court said, and no proof was shown that this was not typical of the Chicago population. Then the Court added this: "Absent clear evidence of general fame or notoriety in the community, and pervasive involvement in the affairs of society, an individual should not be deemed a public personality for all aspects of his life."[31] The message was, simply, that the media must present "clear evidence" that an individual was a public figure. This evidence was not shown in the *Gertz* case, and he was declared a private individual.

As a private individual, the Court said, Gertz did not have to prove a knowing or reckless falsehood at his trial. In this respect the court of appeals was overruled. However, Gertz had been awarded $50,000 in compensatory damages at his trial without proving he had been injured. And *American Opinion* had been held to strict liability, without a showing of fault being required. As a result, the case was sent back for a new trial under these standards.[32]

The Court's formulation of these new standards for private individuals came in an opinion written by one of its new members,

Justice Lewis F. Powell, Jr. It had been endorsed by another new member, Justice William H. Rehnquist, along with Justices Potter Stewart and Thurgood Marshall, whose positions were consistent with that they had expressed in the *Rosenbloom* case. The opinion was given force of law by Justice Harry Blackmun, who had been among the *Rosenbloom* plurality advocating the "public issues" standard.

In a separate opinion, Justice Blackmun said he sensed some illogic in leaving the states free to define what he characterized as a "negligence" standard. But he joined the private-person libel standard, he said, for two reasons. The first was the limitation of damages to actual injuries, which he said should give "sufficient and adequate breathing space for a vigorous press."[33] The second was to allow "the Court to come to rest in the defamation area" with a clearly defined majority position.

The way the law came to rest, however, brought four dissenting opinions. Chief Justice Warren Burger said the Court should have left the law alone with respect to private citizens because that law had been an "orderly development with a consistent basic rationale."[34] The new negligence standard, he said, defied understanding. Justice White also was critical of what he called ill-considered "judicial overkill" and "razing" of state common law of libel.[35] He said the common citizen deserved "considerably more protection" than they would be allowed under the new privilege granted the media.[36]

At the other side of the spectrum, Justice William J. Brennan, Jr., said the latitude of the fault standard, which he said states would probably place at reasonable care, could become an instrument of suppression. Further, he said the wide range of "actual injury" damages could be used by juries to punish unpopular views and hence not allow "the necessary elbow room for First Amendment expression."[37] Agreement here was voiced by Justice William O. Douglas, who said at minimum the Constitution prohibits all libel damages in discussion of public affairs.[38] He stated the Court's struggle to accommodate press freedom with defamation was "a quite hopeless one."[39]

An accommodation, though, had been made, and despite the Court's retreat from the public issue rationale, the area of libel had been considerably diminished. In the decade between 1964 and 1974, the Supreme Court had greatly enlarged the concept of press freedom under the First Amendment. With the *Gertz* decision, private individuals could obtain redress only for actual injury when, at a minimum, they proved defamatory falsehoods were published with fault or negligence. Meanwhile public figures and public officials had to meet a higher actual malice standard, proof of a calculated falsehood or proof of a reckless falsehood despite "subjective awareness of probably falsity."[40] Further, all presumed or punitive damages required proof that publications were made with knowledge of falsity or reckless disregard of whether they were true or false.

One "issue" area also remained in which the knowing or reckless falsehood had to be proved to obtain a libel judgment. This was the labor dispute issue. The Court reiterated this point in another libel decision, *Old Dominion Branch No. 496, National Association of Letter Carriers, AFL-CIO* v. *Austin,* handed down the same day the *Gertz* decision was issued.[41]

The letter carrier case arose when a newsletter of the Richmond, Virginia, branch of the union was published with a "List of Scabs." The list was accompanied by a Jack London article calling "scabs" men of "low character" and "rotten principles" who were traitors to God, country, and family. Three of those named, who had refused to join the union, filed a libel action under the Virginia "insulting words" statute, and each won $55,000 in damages at the trial. These damages were awarded after the trial court judge had instructed jurors that they could, in a labor libel case, find "actual malice" existed with ill will, personal spite, or desire to injure the three postmen.

On review, the erroneous interpretation was attacked by the Supreme Court. In a decision written by Justice Marshall, the Court said that actual malice could be found *only* when there was a knowing or reckless falsehood. Further, the Court said, both Executive Order 11491, governing union-government relations, and the National Labor Relations Act required uninhibited and robust discussion in labor-management relations. In this regard, the Jack London definitions of "scab" were called merely rhetorical hyperbole. Repeating and broadening its decision of the 1966 case, *Linn* v. *United Plant Guard Workers,* the Court said proof of knowing or reckless falsehoods would have to be made concerning any discussion during the ongoing efforts of unions in organizing remaining nonunion employees, even without a specific recognition or election campaign.[42]

The inconsistency of this 6–3 decision with that rendered in *Gertz* was pointed out by the dissenters. The dissenters were Justice Powell, who wrote the *Gertz* majority opinion, and Chief Justice Burger and Justice Rehnquist. They argued that the *Gertz* standard should apply to the case. Powell's dissenting opinion complained about the expansive application of the actual malice standard to ongoing organizing discussions as well as labor disputes. This, he wrote, allowed "both unions and employers to defame individual workers with little or no risk of being held accountable for doing so."[43]

Summary

The Court in these two decisions had, in effect, granted a special segment of the population more protection for discussion of private individuals than it had granted the media. The incongruity is striking when consideration is given to the fact that the grant of discussion to those in union disputes came from a federal law while the basis of the press decision came from what should have been paramount law, the Constitution. Further, the libel standard concerning labor issues was pretty solidly defined, while that for the media was now extremely hazy. For example, the line between public figures and private individuals, while stated, was by no means determinative. Additionally, damages for actual injury, considering that this could be injury to reputation or standing in the community or for personal humiliation or for mental anguish and suffering, provided wide jury discretion. And the "competent evidence" standard for damages simply lacked definition. Above all, though, states were left free to determine their own level of fault, which in itself could allow no uniformity of judgments across the nation.

Still, the burden of proof in all libel cases had been shifted to those filing suit. Publishers and broadcasters—who by legal definition included everyone who dissiminated or made defamatory material known publicly[44]—were no longer held to strict proof of truth for allegedly defamatory statements. Instead, fault had to be proved by those claiming defamatory falsehoods. Additionally, the Court had said there was no such thing as liability for a false opinion. It said ideas—not Courts—countered ideas. Also punitive and presumed damages had been eliminated for everyone without proof of the calculated or reckless falsehood.

The Court's accommodation from one perspective, then, had greatly enhanced press freedom by granting a second, though limited, constitutional privilege for discussing individuals. Further, this second constitutional privilege was a minimum standard. While there could be no liability without fault, states had the latitude to require tougher standards. And some did. After *Gertz,* two of the early state decisions, in Indiana and Colorado, retained the knowing and reckless falsehood standard that had been established in *Rosenbloom* v. *Metromedia.*[45] Some states also adopted a gross negligence test.[46] But the general holding in lower courts was that private individuals had to prove only simple negligence on the part of publishers who circulated defamatory falsehoods.[47] This generally required that a preponderance of the evidence show the lack of care that a reasonably prudent man would have used in like circumstances.[48]

Prudence also was required of lower court judges in the task of separating private from public figures. In *Gertz* the Court had strongly indicated that those who bring libel suits were to be declared private individuals unless "clear evidence" was presented to show that they were public figures. It had further warned that public figures "for all purposes and all contexts" were few. Room was left by the Court, however, for private individuals to be termed public figures if they were voluntarily thrust into public controversies to influence the issues involved. Questions were raised, however, about involuntary participation. The Court also had noticeably stressed a criterion of involvement in public "controversies," not in the "issues of concern to the public" that former Chief Justice Earl Warren had stressed in *Curtis Publishing Co.* v. *Butts.*[49]

These, then, were the guidelines. And whether or not there had been a subtle retrenchment in the "public-figure" designation simply was not clear. Hence the task facing lower court judges in separating private- from public-person plaintiffs was not easy. This was quickly seen by widely varying decisions.[50] One federal judge, pointing to the "nebulous concepts" involved, described distinguishing between private people and public figures as "much like trying to nail a jellyfish to the wall."[51]

Such distinctions, though, were all important—both for individuals bringing libel actions and for those defending them. If a judge ruled a public figure was involved, liability for a defamatory falsehood depending on clear and convincing proof that publication was made with knowledge of falsity or reckless disregard for falsity. If it was ruled that the plaintiff was a private individual, liability likely rested on proof only by a preponderance of the evidence that the falsehood was published negligently and that actual injury was involved. Two quite different constitutional privileges prevailed to limit the scope of libel.

9/ A Constitutional Accommodation
Libel Recovery Clearly Is Not Foreclosed

Though the Supreme Court between 1964 and 1974 had greatly limited the conditions under which all people could obtain redress for defamatory falsehoods, it had not granted a license for unlimited libelous discussion. What had been granted were constitutional privileges to speak or publish only nonknowing or nonreckless defamatory falsehoods about public officials and public figures and only nonnegligent defamatory falsehoods about private individuals. Obviously these privileges could be defeated by proof of knowing, reckless, or negligent falsehoods. There was, then, no freedom for unlimited libelous discussion. The Court simply had made a constitutional accommodation between freedom of speech and press, on the one hand, and the right of individuals to maintain good reputations, on the other. Room was left by this accommodation to allow damage awards to those injured by libelous falsehoods not protected by the Constitution. And as the decade of the 1970s closed out, the Court made this quite clear by issuing several decisions emphasizing that the rights of those filing libel suits would be protected.

The first of these decisions came nearly two years after the private-person rule of libel had been established in *Gertz* v. *Welch*. It was in the case of *Time, Inc.,* v. *Firestone,* decided on 2 March 1976. Here the Court in a 5–3 opinion said, in effect, that wealthy, socially prominent people—even if they had frequent media attention—were not to be considered public figures for purposes of libel suits unless they had assumed special prominence in the resolution of public questions. Nor could they be termed public figures by being compelled to go to court, even if their trials were highly publicized and they had several press conferences concerning them.[1] Rather they were to be considered private individuals who had to prove defamatory falsehoods about them were published with fault, not with knowledge of falsity or reckless disregard of falsity.

This case arose when Mrs. Firestone, a wealthy socialite whose affairs frequently were reported by the media but were determinative of no public issues, filed a libel action against *Time* magazine. *Time* had published the following article in its "Milestone" section: "DIVORCED. By Russell A. Firestone, Jr., heir to the tire fortune: Mary Alice Sullivan Firestone, 32, his third wife; a onetime Palm Beach school teacher; on grounds of extreme cruelty and adultery; after six years of marriage, one son; in West Palm Beach, Fla. The 17-month intermittent trial produced enough testimony of extramarital adventures on both sides, said the judge, 'to make Dr. Freud's hair curl.' " The article had been based on Russell Firestone's petition for divorce, which had alleged extreme cruelty and adultery, and on the fact that the judge had ruled that Firestone's petition "for divorce be and the same is hereby granted." The ruling was hazy, but the outward basis for the divorce appeared clear. Florida law, however, did not allow alimony on a finding of adultery. And the judge also had granted Mrs. Firestone alimony of $3,000 a month. Hence she claimed *Time* falsely libeled her. A jury agreed, rejecting *Time*'s contention that the report was accurate. *Time* was held to strict liability under Florida law, and negligence in this pre-*Gertz* trial was not an issue. Mrs. Firestone won a $100,000 libel judgment.

On appeal, an intermediate Florida court overturned the judgment, in part, on a finding that *Time* had fairly reported the divorce judgment.[2] But the Florida Supreme Court disagreed, saying if adultery had been found, there could be no alimony. Further the Florida high court said the divorce was based on lack of "domestication," even though this, too, was not a basis for divorce in Florida. Meanwhile the *Gertz* decision had been rendered, prohibiting damages for falsehoods without a finding of fault, and the Florida Supreme Court attempted to comply with its requirements. It said that *Time*'s erroneous reporting of the judgment, without careful examination of the final divorce decree, was clear and convincing evidence of negligence.[3] Mrs. Firestone's damage award was thus reinstated. And *Time* petitioned the U.S. Supreme Court for review.

The Supreme Court cavalierly rejected *Time*'s argument that Mrs. Firestone should be considered a public figure who had to prove a knowing or reckless falsehood to obtain a libel judgment. The Court, in an opinion written by Justice William H. Rehnquist, said that Mrs. Firestone "did not assume any role of especial prominence in the affairs of society, other than perhaps Palm Beach society, and she did not thrust herself to the forefront of any particular controversy in order to influence the resolution of the issues involved in it."[4] Mrs. Firestone in trying to settle her divorce action, the Court said, was not trying to settle a public controversy, though it may have been a controversy of interest to the public.[5] And private individuals involved in matters of public interest did not have to prove calculated or reckless falsehoods to obtain damages, the Court said, as *Gertz* v. *Welch* had rejected this view. As a private individual, she had to prove only that falsehoods were negligently published.

More damaging for the press, perhaps, was the Court's rejection of *Time*'s claim that there should be no liability for reports of judicial proceedings without proof of a knowing or reckless falsehood. The Court said:

> Imposing upon the law of private defamation the rather drastic limitations worked by *New York Times* cannot be justified by generalized references to the public interest in reports of judicial proceedings. The details of many, if not most, courtroom battles would add almost nothing towards advancing the uninhibited debate on public issues thought to provide principle support for the decision in *New York Times*. . . . And while participants in some litigation may be legitimate "public figures," either generally or for the limited purpose of that litigation, the majority will more likely resemble respondent, drawn into a public forum largely against their will in order to attempt to obtain the only redress available to them or to defend themselves against actions brought by the State or others. There appears little reason why those individuals should substantially forfeit that degree of protection which the law of defamation would otherwise afford them simply by virtue of their being drawn into a courtroom.[6]

In effect, the Court said that the media was liable if negligence was proved in publishing inaccurate, libelous reports of judicial proceedings involving private people. This obviously extended even to liability for negligently misinterpreting judge's decisions in such proceedings.

But the Supreme Court was not convinced that *Time* had been found to be negligent, or at fault. While it held that there was competent evidence of actual injury to support the $100,000 damage award, because of Mrs. Firestone's testimony of "anxiety" and "concern" as to the effect of the adultery charge on her son, fault was another thing. In this respect the Supreme Court refused to accept the Florida Supreme Court's first instance declaration of *Time*'s negligence because it was not "supportably ascertained" by an actual finding of fact that fault did or did not exist. Further, the U.S. Supreme Court refused to make an independent determination of fault by canvassing the record, as it had done in other libel cases. Rather the case was sent back to the state for retrial to determine if *Time*'s account actually was the result of some fault on its part.[7]

Rehnquist's opinion was signed by Chief Justice Warren Burger and Justice Harry Blackmun. And it was joined by Justices Lewis F. Powell, Jr., and Potter Stewart "to avoid the appearance of fragmentation of the Court on the basic principles involved."[8] However both of these justices did canvass the record. They cited the ambiguous divorce judgment and said there was "substantial evidence" that *Time* was not guilty of "actionable negligence."[9]

A dissent by Justice Thurgood Marshall said there was no basis for fault and that Mrs. Firestone, a member of the "sporting set," had achieved "especial prominence in the affairs of society" and should be required to make the harder proofs of a public figure.[10] Another dissent, by Justice Byron R. White, said negligence should not have to be proved in a libel trial that took place before *Gertz*—and that *Time* clearly was at fault anyway.[11] Justice William J. Brennan, Jr., also dissented, saying there should be no liability for libel in judicial proceedings unless calculated or reckless falsehood were proven. He also felt there should have been no damages because there had been no actual showing of reputational harm, as required by the *Gertz* decision.[12]

Again, then, the Court was badly divided. But the message of the majority was clear. Those filing libel suits were private individuals unless their positions were such that they influenced public issues—either in all or limited instances—or unless they attempted to influence some particular public controversy.[13] And a court trial, necessary only because a controversy must be settled by the mechanism of society, was not considered a public controversy. Additionally it made no difference if libelous articles concerning court trials focused on the ruling of judges, who are public officials. No consideration was given by any member of the Court to the theory advanced by Justice White in *Rosenbloom* that actions of public officials—in this case the declaration of a judge—could be discussed without liability, short of the knowing or reckless falsehood, and with no requirement that the reputation of individuals affected by those actions be spared.

Despite the fact that the report was on a government proceeding, the ruling was based strictly on the private-person rule of libel. Further it had become evident in this case that actual injury, the basis of damages in private person suits, could be almost anything relating to injured reputation. Still, the hurdle for private individuals was high. They had to prove at least negligence, along with falsity and defamation. The constitutional privilege of discussion, protected by the First Amendment, had not been ignored even though the Court appeared willing to give libel plaintiffs the benefit of any doubt concerning their status as private individuals and their proofs of actual injury.

Protection for plaintiffs also was underscored in the case of *Herbert* v. *Lando,* which the Court decided on 19 April 1979. This was a $44,725,000 libel action filed by the former army colonel Anthony Herbert, who had achieved national prominence in 1971 when, as commander of a battalion in the 173d Airborne Brigade, he formally accused his superior officers of covering up war crimes in Vietnam. He claimed he was relieved of his command for pressing the charges, and the story was widely publicized. However in 1973, Columbia Broadcasting System, through its television documentary series, *60 Minutes,* broadcast a program entitled "the Selling of Colonel Herbert," which cast doubt on Herbert's allegations. He sued the CBS, program producer Barry Lando, the program correspondent Mike Wallace, and *Atlantic Monthly* magazine, which had published a subsequent Lando article about Herbert.

Herbert claimed the program—by skillful editing and one-sided interviewing—had falsely and deliberately portrayed him as a liar who had fashioned the war crimes charges to explain his dismissal from command.[14] The article, he claimed, was published with knowledge of falsity. Hence he attempted by depositions, in pretrial discovery, to question Lando about his state of mind—his thoughts, conversations, and conclusions—while preparing the broadcast and follow-up story. Lando refused. And before the actual trial of the case, this question went from a U.S. district court to a U.S. appeals court and finally to the Supreme Court. Here it was held that Herbert had every right to inquire into Lando's "state of mind."

The Supreme Court, in a 6 3 opinion written by Justice Byron R. White, had this to say:

New York Times and its progeny made it essential to proving liability that plaintiffs focus on the conduct and state of mind of the defendant. To be liable, the alleged defamer of public officials or of public figures must know or have reason to suspect that his publication is false. In other cases proof of some kind of fault, negligence perhaps, is essential to recovery. Inevitably, unless liability is to be completely foreclosed, the thoughts and editorial processes of the alleged defamer would be open to examination.

It is also untenable to conclude from our cases that although proof of the necessary state of mind could be in the form of objective circumstances from which the ultimate fact could be inferred, plaintiffs may not inquire directly from the defendants whether they knew or had reason to suspect that their damaging publication was in error.[15]

In short, the Court said it would not "place beyond the plaintiff's reach a range of direct evidence relevant to proving knowing or reckless falsehood by the publisher of an alleged libel."[16] This was true, the Court emphasized, whether the private-individual plaintiff had to prove a negligent falsehood or a public figure-official plaintiff had to prove a knowing or reckless falsehood.

Also there could be no privilege for the media, according to the opinion, to eliminate editorial processes from inquiry by those bringing libel actions and seeking evidence. Otherwise it would "place beyond reach what the defendant participants learned or knew as the result of such collegiate conversations or exchanges." The Court also said: "It may be that plaintiff will rarely be successful in proving awareness of falsehood from the mouth of the defendant himself, but the relevance of answers to such inquiries . . . can hardly be doubted. To erect an impenetrable barrier to the plaintiff's use of such evidence on his side of the case is a matter of some substance, particularly when defendants themselves are prone to assert their good faith belief in the truth of their publications, and libel plaintiffs are required to prove knowing or reckless falsehood with 'convincing clarity.' "[17] Further no law was changed, the Court said, by requiring that editorial processes or "state of mind" be open to inquiry. This had been asserted in *Gertz v. Welch*, was at issue in *Curtis Publishing Co. v. Butts,* and had been mentioned in *New York Times v. Sullivan.*[18] The Court even listed some forty state libel cases in the footnotes to show that evidence concerning editorial processes had been offered through the years to determine malice or lack of malice in common-law libel trials.[19]

Interestingly, none of the dissenters questioned inquiries into mental processes of those accused of libel. They did, however, claim that some protection for editorial conferences of journalists before broadcast or publication was essential. Justices Marshall and Stewart would have completely foreclosed "discovery in defamation cases as to the substance of editorial conversation."[20] Justice Brennan would have done the same unless a prima facie case had been made that the alleged libel was a defamatory falsehood.[21] All justices, then, saw knowledge of falsity as turning on the state of mind of the defendants and recognized the validity of inquiries by those bringing libel suits.

Nevertheless, when the Supreme Court sent the case back to the trial level, with instructions that state-of-mind inquiries were proper in pretrial discovery, a storm of protest came from the media.[22] For example, Allen Neuharth, then president of the American Newspaper Publishers Association, accused "the imperial judiciary . . . that is bending the First Amendment at every turn" of creating an "atmosphere of intimidation."[23] The widespread protest eventually prompted Justice Brennan, a staunch advocate of press freedom, to retaliate in a public speech. He said: "It would hardly be fair to say that a plaintiff can only recover if he establishes intentional falsehood and at the same time to say that he cannot inquire into a defendant's intentions."[24] His contention was that the decision deserved a more considered response from the press. This also was the opinion of a number of news media lawyers, who felt the decision was of minor legal significance.[25] About the only thing the decision really did was instruct those bringing libel suits in how to go about gathering evidence for their cases.

Similarly, instructions for judges appeared to be the primary thrust of the next two libel decisions, rendered on 26 June 1979. These cases, *Wolston v. Reader's Digest* and *Hutchinson v. Proxmire*, again focused on the distinction between private individuals and public figures. Rulings by the specific lower court judges, to the effect that the plaintiffs in these cases were public figures, were overturned. And again the Supreme Court indicated that the public-figure category, for the purposes of libel suits, was indeed quite narrow.

Wolston v. Reader's Digest stemmed from a book published in 1974 about the Soviet Union's espionage activities since World War II. The book, entitled *KGB: The Secret Work of Soviet Agents,* listed Ilya Wolston as being among seventeen "Soviet agents who were convicted of espionage or falsifying information or perjury and/or contempt charges following espionage indictments." The index of the book also referred to him as a "Soviet agent in U.S." But Wolston had never been indicted for espionage as the book stated. And he brought suit for libel against the publisher, *Reader's Digest,* the author, John Barron, and subsequent publishers of the book.

The case was not so simplistic, however. Wolston, a Russian-born immigrant who had lived in the United States since 1939 and who had worked in different government jobs, domestic and foreign, was a nephew of confessed Soviet spies Jack and Myra Sobel. At the time of their arrest in 1957, Wolston was questioned by the Federal Bureau of Investigation. Shortly after this he was ordered to testify several times before a federal grand jury in New York during a widely publicized investigation of Soviet spying in the United States. On one occasion, in 1958, he failed to appear when subpoenaed to testify—because of what he said was poor health. As a result, a federal judge held him in contempt of court and placed him on probation for three years, conditioned upon cooperation with the grand jury in its investigation. He was convincted for contempt, but *not* after an indictment for espionage. Nevertheless he received considerable media attention at the time. And in a later report prepared by the FBI in May 1960, he was listed among people "the F.B.I. investigation resulted in identifying as Soviet intelligence agents."[26]

Because of all this, when Wolston filed his suit, *Reader's Digest* claimed he was a public figure for the purpose of comment on his connection with Soviet espionage in the 1950s. The district court judge agreed, held there was no showing of a calculated or reckless falsehood, and granted *Reader's Digest* summary judgment. This was affirmed by the U.S. Court of Appeals for the District of Columbia.[27] However, the United States Supreme Court held that Wolston was not a public figure and hence was not required to prove a knowing or reckless falsehood to receive damages for libel.

Pointing out that Wolston had led a "thoroughly private existence" before the grand jury investigation and later returned to obscurity, the Court said he had achieved no especial prominence in affairs of society and hence was not a public figure of "pervasive power and influence."[28] Also, the Court said, he did not thrust himself into the Soviet spy controversy to influence the outcome of issues involved.[29] More accurately, it was stated, Wolston was "dragged unwillingly into the controversy" by the contempt citation.[30] Then, in an 8–1 opinion, written by Justice William Rehnquist, the Court said:

It is clear that petitioner played only a minor role in whatever public controversy there may have been concerning the investigation of Soviet espionage. We decline to hold that his mere citation for contempt rendered him a public figure for purposes of comment on the investigation of Soviet espionage.

Petitioner's failure to appear before the grand jury and citation for contempt no doubt were "newsworthy," but the simple fact that the events attracted media attention also is not conclusive of the public figure issue. A private individual is not automatically transformed into a public figure just by becoming involved in or associated with a matter that attracts public attention. To accept such reasoning would in effect re-establish the doctrine advanced by the plurality in *Rosenbloom* v. *Metromedia, Inc.*[31]

Wolston, according to the Court, had retained his private person status and had in no way relinquished his right in the protection of his "own name" by being drawn into a public issue.[32]

However, the Court went further than Wolston's "own name," stating: "This reasoning leads us to reject the further contention of respondent that any person who engages in criminal conduct automatically becomes a public figure for purposes of comment on a limited range of issues relating to his conviction."[33] The Court here conspicuously ignored the fact that an individual's criminal conduct, by definition,[34] thrusts him beyond his "own" rights into those of the general public.

Instead, the opinion reiterated the *Time, v. Firestone* doctrine that while some court trials would involve legitimate public figures, most likely would involve private individuals there against their will. "To hold otherwise," the Court said, "would create an "open season" for all who sought to defame persons convicted of a crime."[35] This language, indicating the media seeks people to defame, was described by at least one commentator at the time as being "merely unbelievable."[36] But giving the phrase its very best interpretation, the media was put on notice that neither criminal defendants in court nor those convicted of crimes were automatically to be considered public figures.

In Wolston's particular case, the Court said he was entitled to recover in a new trial if he could prove fault in publication of a defamatory falsehood. This brought agreement in a separate opinion by Justices Blackmun and Marshall, but they disagreed with the reasoning for Wolston being a private individual. They in effect said he may have been a public figure for purposes of contemporaneous reporting in 1958 but that he had lost his public-figure status in 1974 by passage of time.[37] Only Justice Brennan dissented, and even he felt there should have been no summary judgment because, in his opinion, a genuine issue of fact existed as to a calculated or reckless falsehood.[38] Despite the divisions, then, all justices disagreed with Wolston's treatment in lower courts.

Another 8–1 opinion was issued by the Supreme Court in the case of *Hutchinson* v. *Proxmire*, decided on the same day. This was an $8 million libel action filed by Dr. Ronald Hutchinson, a research scientist, against the United States senator William Proxmire and his legislative assistant, Morton Schwartz. Senator Proxmire in April 1975, had presented his Golden Fleece of the Month Award to several federal agencies that had spent upward of $500,000 on Hutchinson's research on emotional behavior, some of which had centered on animals. The awards were for what Proxmire considered wasteful spending. He made a speech in the Senate and repeated his comments in a press release and newsletter, stating: "Dr. Hutchinson's studies should make the taxpayers as well as his monkeys grind their teeth. In fact, the good doctor has made a fortune from his monkeys and in the process has made a monkey out of the American taxpayer."³⁹ At the time, Hutchinson was a government employee, serving as director of research at the Kalamazoo State Mental Hospital in Michigan. However he shifted jobs to a nonprofit organization some two months later and kept the research funding, which was provided in hopes of solving problems of individuals being confined in close quarters in undersea and space experiments. After Hutchinson's job shift, Proxmire appeared on television programs and referred to the research but not to Hutchinson. Finally in early 1976 Proxmire sent out another newsletter stating: "All the studies on why monkeys clench their jaws were dropped. No more monkey business."⁴⁰

Hutchinson sued. In answer, Proxmire asked for a summary judgment on the claim that his acts and utterances were protected by the Speech and Debate Clause of the Constitution and that criticism of spending was protected by the First Amendment. Further, he asserted that Hutchinson was both a public figure and a public official and would have to prove a calculated or reckless falsehood. The U.S. district judge agreed with all Proxmire's contentions and granted him a summary judgment. This was affirmed by the court of appeals, which upheld Proxmire's congressional immunity claim. The appeals court did say that a defamatory falsehood may have been in the press release claiming Hutchinson had made a personal fortune and the research was possibly duplicative. But Hutchinson was a public figure, the appeals court said, and there was no evidence of a knowing or reckless falsehood. The appellate decision did not consider the public-official claim.

On review, the Supreme Court overruled the lower courts. In the first place, the Court said, Proxmire had no privilege to defame others "under color of a performance of the duties of his office" unless in committee or house proceedings.⁴¹ A speech in the Senate or printed in the *Congressional Record* would be immune to liability, the Court said, but newsletters and press releases were not part of the deliberative process.⁴² Also the Court discounted the duty of those in Congress to inform the public of their activities. In an opinion written by Chief Justice Burger, the Court said: "Valuable and desirable as it may be in broad terms, the transmittal of such information by individual Members in order to inform the public and other Members is not a part of the legislative function or the deliberations that make up the legislative process. As a result transmittal of such information by press releases and newsletters is not protected by the Speech and Debate Clause."[43] It was thus ruled that Senator Proxmire would have to go to court to defend himself against the libel action.

And for the purpose of that suit, the Court ruled that Hutchinson was not a public figure. He did not have such access to the media as to warrant such designation, the Court said, and he had assumed no role of public prominence in the broad question of concern about government spending.[44] The only thing that brought him to public attention was the Golden Fleece Award, which was claimed to be libelous. The Court said: "Hutchinson did not thrust himself or his views into public controversy to influence others. Respondents have not identified such a particular controversy; at most they point to a concern about general public expenditures. But that concern is shared by most and relates to most public expenditures; it is not sufficient to make Hutchinson a public figure. If it were, everyone who received or benefited from the myriad public grants for research could be classified as a public figure—a conclusion that our previous opinions have rejected."[45] Involvement in a matter of public interest again was rejected by the Court as a basis for the "public-figure" designation.

However, the Court expressed no opinion on whether Hutchinson, a public employee at the time of the Proxmire award, should be termed a public official. While the district court had made such a finding, it had not been considered by the court of appeals. Hence the Supreme Court said the issue was not before it. In a footnote, though, it was made clear that the precise boundaries for the public-official designation had not been determined. "It cannot be thought to include all public employees, however," the Court said.[46]

This statement cast uncertainties and carried implications not only for Senator Proxmire's new trial but for the entire public-official rule of libel. The Court in the 1966 case of *Rosenblatt* v. *Baer* had ruled that government employees were public officials if perceived by the public as having substantial responsibility for control over the conduct of government affairs.[47] And this definition had worked effectively for more than a decade in libel suits throughout the nation. Yet the Court here, in *Hutchinson* v. *Prox-mire,* appeared by footnote to be giving a signal that reconsideration was due.

Even more ominous was a footnote in the decision questioning summary judgments, which the Court specifically had endorsed in three previous cases.[48] In fact, in *Rosenblatt,* the Court had ruled that judges, not jurors, should determine who was a public official along with "other questions of privilege generally."[49] But here, in *Proxmire,* the Court's footnote stated: "Considering the nuances of the issues raised here, we are constrained to express some doubt about the so-called 'rule.' The proof of 'actual malice' calls a defendant's state of mind into question . . . and does not really lend itself to summary disposition."[50] This, too, possibly forewarned of a shift that would greatly affect the media, which relied heavily on summary judgments to prevent costly court trials in cases where showing of proof clearly did not meet constitutional standards of privilege.

A careful reader, though, would have to question the footnotes in Chief Justice Burger's opinion. One was completely illogical, stating the Court had never determined specifically that the knowing and reckless falsehood standard applied to an individual defendant as opposed to a media defendant. This ignored *Garrison* v. *Louisiana,* in which an individual district attorney had issued press releases, much like Proxmire.[51] Also it ignored *St. Amant* v. *Thompson.*[52] Phil A. St. Amant was an individual defendant, much like Proxmire. The only difference was that St. Amant was seeking a Senate seat, which Proxmire already held.

The footnotes, though, were endorsed by eight members of the Court and could not be discounted. While they did not have the force of law, they did have meaning, possibly as indicators. And they could be interpreted as readiness by the Supreme Court to back away from some protections that clearly had been sanctioned for the media and others in previous decisions.

Summary

As the last quarter of the twentieth century dawned, then, the Supreme Court appeared to be saying that while constitutional privileges of discussion had been recognized, the media—and even members of Congress—would be held to tight accountability for perceived abuses of those privileges. All areas of doubt in libel decisions, following the Court's swing in *Gertz* v. *Welch,* had been resolved by the Burger Court in favor of protection for individual reputation as opposed to protection for "robust, uninhibited, wide-open" discussion. In this respect, there had been a definite retrenchment in Court philosophy.

The retrenchment was noticeable in other ways as well. Following *Herbert* v. *Lando,* in which it was held that those bringing libel suits could inquire into publishers' "state of mind," the Court obliquely questioned the appropriateness of judges issuing summary judgments in constitutional libel cases. Also whether by intention or happenstance, the Court injected confusion—by footnote—into its previously announced rule for determining whether public employees were public officials. And in *Time, Inc.,* v. *Firestone,* where the fault standard was at issue, a divided majority of the Court even backed away from its previous practice in libel cases of making an independent review of the record to determine if liability actually existed. Even further, the Court indicated a willingness to accept any testimony of harm from a plaintiff as sufficient to meet its requirement that there be competent evidence of actual injury for a damage award.

The most telling constriction, though, came with the lines drawn by the Court between private individuals and public figures. Lower court determinations, made in good faith attempts to follow what were believed to be established guidelines, were repeatedly being struck down. The Court appeared to ignore the statement in *Gertz* that individuals could be drawn into public controversies and hence be involuntary public figures. Instead, the public-figure status was narrowly confined by these decisions. It could be conferred only to those who had "assumed roles of especial prominence in society," which the Court seemed to limit to those with "pervasive power and influence," either in all or limited issues, *and* to those who "thrust themselves into the forefront of particular public controversies in order to influence the resolution of issues involved."

Moreover, public controversies were narrowly defined. It did not, the Court said, include controversies of interest to the public such as court trials. Though by any definition trials were to settle controversies no longer private, those voluntarily or involuntarily drawn into them could not automatically be considered public figures. It did not matter that criminal charges might be involved, or that official government actions were being reported. Those engaged in criminal conduct, the Court said, could not automatically be considered public figures. Additionally, the Court specifically had refused public-figure status for a defendant to a criminal charge related to an investigation furor over spy activities, to a government research scientist receiving large public grants questioned by a U.S. senator, and to a wealthy socialite who had received widespread media attention. They had not tried to determine issues, the Court said. They were simply involved in issues.

It was clear that the Burger Court was signaling judges everywhere that involvement in issues was not enough to make plaintiffs public figures. Some of the particular decisions brought disagreement within the Court, sometimes within the majority itself. Obviously a precise "boundary" problem still existed between private individuals and others—specifically as to when public employees became public officials and when individuals reached that hazy "especial prominence" to become public figures. Nevertheless, the Court had made a conscious decision not to allow "open season," as Justice Rehnquist called it, on the great majority of people in the United States. More specifically, the Court had determined that its judically determined constitutional privileges of discussion should not foreclose recovery for libel.

The message was clear—to judges, lawyers, and those in the media. This was shown by the decisions that followed in the lower courts, by the increase in the number of libel suits that were filed, and by the jump in libel insurance policies purchased by newspapers and broadcasting companies.[53] One computer check in 1979, the year of this last series of Supreme Court decisions, even showed that the number of libel actions filed in federal courts was 51 percent greater than those filed in 1975 after the *Gertz* decision.[54] Also lower courts noticeably tightened up on the public-figure designation.[55] And while summary judgments protecting the media from frivolous suits still appeared to be common, a few courts refused such judgments, relying on the Burger footnote questioning the "rule."[56]

Still, freedom of speech and press had been greatly enhanced by the Court since the 1964 *New York Times v. Sullivan* decision. The Burger Court had made subtle changes, but the basic rules still held. Public officials and public figures had to prove actual malice, defined as a knowing or reckless falsehood, to obtain damages for defamation. Private individuals, the bulk of the population, had to prove that defamatory falsehoods about them were communicated with fault, probably negligence, depending on the individual states. With these rules, considerable "breathing space" had been given for even libelous falsehoods, inevitable in the open discussion necessary for democracy. While the Burger Court obviously had tried to balance the scales to protect individuals, the constitutional privileges of discussion nevertheless still existed.

NOTES

TABLE OF CASES

INDEX

NOTES

Preface

1. Oliver Wendell Holmes, Jr., *The Common Law* (Boston: Little, Brown and Company, 43d print., 1949), pp. 1–2, 35–36. Also see Oliver Wendell Holmes, *Collected Legal Papers* (New York: Peter Smith, 1952), p. 129.

Prologue

1. Case de Libellis Famosis, 5 Coke Reports 125A at 125B (1606).
2. Ibid., p. 125A.
3. Ibid., p. 125B.
4. Rex v. Udall (1590), 1 *Howell's State Trials* 1271 at 1283, 1289; Rex v. Twyn (1663), 6 *Howell's State Trials* 701 at 709. Twyn was hanged, cut down alive, and his body cut into quarters. His head and body were placed over gates to London.
5. Nathaniel B. Shurtleff, ed., *Records of the Governor and Company of the Massachusetts Bay in New England* (Boston: William White Co., 1835), 1:160–61, with accounts of letters, pp. 156–58.
6. George Keith, *New-England's Spirit of Persecution Transmitted to Pennsylvania: and the Pretended Quaker Found Persecuting the True Christian-Quaker, in the Tryal of Peter Boss, George Keith, Thomas Budd and William Bradford* (New York, 1693), pp. 33, 34. Also see *The Proprietor v. George Keith, William Bradford, Thomas Budd, and Peter Boss,* in Samuel W. Pennypacker, *Pennsylvania Colonial Cases* (Philadelphia: Rees Welsch and Co., Law Book Publishers, 1892), p. 117–44.
7. Pennypacker, *Pennsylvania Colonial Cases,* p. 125.
8. Theo Philanthes, *New-England Persecutors Mauled with Their Own Weapons* (New York, 1697), pp. 58, 60, 61, 62.
9. J. W. Fortescue, ed., *Calendar of State Papers, Colonial Series, America*

and West Indies, October 1697–December 1698, Preserved in the Public Record Office (London: Her Majesty's Stationers Offices, 1905; reprinted at Vadiz: Kraus Reprint Ltd., 1964), 16:329, 399. Also see entries on p. 413, secs. 422, 654, 762, 790, and 812.

10. Ibid., p. 503. Other entries involving the incident are on pp. 154, 161, 166, 169, 205, 392, 407, 420, 525, 526, and 529.

11. Isaiah Thomas, *The History of Printing in America, with a Biography of Printers, and an Account of Newspapers* (Albany, N.Y.: Joel Mansell, printer for American Antiquarian Society, 1874), 2:220.

12. The case was reprinted in colonial and English newspapers and was reported in 17 *Howell's State Trials* at 675–747, because it had, the editor said, "made a general noise in the world." However, the editor also stated that "the decision is not allowed by the courts to be the law here [in England]."

13. Ibid., p. 722.

14. Ibid., p. 723.

15. James Alexander, *A Brief Narrative of the Case and Trial of John Peter Zenger, Printer of the New-York Weekly Journal* (New York: W. Dunlap, 1756), pp. 37–39.

16. Thomas, *The History of Printing*, 2:48; George Henry Payne, *History of Journalism in the United States* (1920; reprint ed., Westport, Conn.: Greenwood Press, 1970), p. 70.

17. Thomas, *The History of Printing*, 1:333–34.

18. Among those called to account before assemblies were Daniel Fowle, Andrew Bradford, Hugh Gaine, and James Parker. Thorough discussions of suppression through legislative action can be found in Leonard W. Levy, *Freedom of the Press from Zenger to Jefferson* (New York: Bobbs-Merrill Co., Inc., 1966).

19. See account of Justice Thomas Hutchinson's problems in Massachusetts in Josiah Quincy, Jr., *Reports of Cases Argued and Adjudged in the Superior Court of Judicature of the Province of Massachusetts Bay between 1761 and 1772* (Boston: Little, Brown and Co., 1865), pp. 260–70, 305.

20. Thomas, *The History of Printing*, 1:168.

21. Arthur M. Schlesinger, *Prelude to Independence* (New York: Alfred A. Knopf, 1958), pp. 115, 116. Schlesinger cites the *Gazette* of 2 June 1770 and the *New York Journal* of 19 April 1770. The pamphlet was *A Brief Narrative of the Case and Trial of John Peter Zenger* (New York: John Holt, 1770).

22. Jonathan Blenman, *Remarks on Zenger's Trial* (New York: Hugh Gaine, 1770).

23. A more detailed account of all the cases mentioned in this prologue can

be found in Clifton O. Lawhorne, *Defamation and Public Officials: The Evolving Law of Libel* (Carbondale and Edwardsville: Southern Illinois University Press, 1971), pp. 1–37. In England jurors could not determine libel until 1793 with Fox's Libel Act, 31 Geo. 3, c. 60; truth did not excuse libel until 1843 with Lord Campbell's Act, *Stats.* 6 and 7, Vict., c. 96, sec. 6.

1. Early Views of the Constitution
States Not Bound by Free Press Guarantee

1. Thomas James Norton, *The Constitution of the United States: Its Sources and Its Application* (New York: Committee for Constitutional Government, Inc., 1960), pp. 194, 196; Edward G. Hudon, *Freedom of Speech and Press in America* (Washington, D.C.: Public Affairs Press, 1963), p. 5.

2. U.S., *Constitution*, Amend. 1.

3. Charles Warren, *A History of the American Bar* (New York: Howard Fertig, Inc., 1966), p. 237; Gerald J. Baldasty, "Toward an Understanding of the First Amendment: Boston Newspapers 1782–1791," *Journalism History* 3, no. 1 (Spring 1976): 25; "Original Draft of Letter from William Cushing, Chief Justice, to Hon. John Adams," *Massachusetts Law Quarterly* 27, no. 4 (October 1942): 16.

4. The trial of Edmund Freeman in Boston for libel, *Herald of Freedom*, 11 March 1791, p. 2; 18 March 1791, p. 1; 25 March 1791, p. 1. "The Trial of William Cobbett for Libel, Philadelphia, Penn., 1797," in John D. Lawson, *American State Trials* (Saint Louis: H. H. Thomas Law Book Co., 1916), 6:675–86. Also libel prosecution dropped against Eleazer Oswald, Respublica v. Oswald, 1 Dall 318 at 320 (U.S. 1788).

5. See Francis Newton Thorpe, *Federal and State Constitutions, Colonial Charters and Other Organic Laws* (Washington, D.C.: Government Printing Office, 1909), 5:3, 100 for Pennsylvania Constitution of 1790; 5:465 for Delaware Constitution of 1792; 3:1274 for Kentucky Constitution of 1792; 6:3 for Tennessee Constitution of 1792, all of which refuted the common law of seditious libel in England.

6. United States v. Worrall, 2 Dall. 374 at 393–94 (U.S. 1798).

7. *Congressional Globe* (House), 5 Cong., 2 sess. (Washington, D.C.: Gales and Seaton, 1851), pp. 2139–71.

8. 1 *Stat.* 20–21.

9. Attorney General v. Zenger, 17 *Howell's State Trials* 675 at 707, 720, 722.

10. Thomas Cooper, *Treatise on the Law of Libel and Liberty of the Press* (reprint ed., New York: G. F. Hopkins, 1930), p. 78; Edward Channing,

History of the United States (New York: Macmillan Co., 1917), 4:232; Clifton O. Lawhorne, *Defamation and Public Officials: The Evolving Law of Libel* (Carbondale and Edwardsville: Southern Illinois University Press, 1971), p. 52, specifically, with detailed discussion of the Sedition Law prosecutions, pp. 39–56.

11. Jonathan Elliot, ed., *The Debates in the Several State Conventions on the Adoption of the Federal Constitution . . . and Other Illustrations of the Constitution* (Philadelphia, 1896), 4:553–54.

12. United States v. Callendar, 25 F. Cas. at 251 (No. 14,790) (1800); United States v. Haswell, 26 F. Cas. 218 (5 May 1800). Also see Albert J. Beveridge, *The Life of John Marshall* (New York: Houghton Mifflin Co., 1919), 3:32, 194.

13. United States v. Callender, 25 F. Cas. 239, app. on Chase's impeachment trial, p. 258.

14. After Jefferson assumed the presidency, he pardoned all who had been convicted under the law. Blair and Rives, *The Congressional Globe, 26th Cong. 1st sess., Dec. 2–July 21, 1839–40* (Washington, D.C.: Globe Office, 1840), p. 412. Also see Jefferson's letter to Mrs. John Adams, Albert Ellen Beyh, ed., *The Writings of Thomas Jefferson* (Washington, D.C.: The Jefferson Memorial Association, 1907), 11:43–44.

15. Lawhorne, *Defamation*, pp. 52–69; some specific cases include Commonwealth v. Clapp, 4 Mass. 163 (1808); Respublica v. Dennis, 2 Am. Dec. 402 (Pa. 1803); Commonwealth v. Morris, 5 Am. Dec. 515 (Va. 1811); *Rush v. Cobbett, Report of an Action for Libel* (Philadelphia: W. W. Woodward, 1800), pamphlet.

16. Constitutional provisions for a defense of truth can be found in Thorp, *Constitutions*, vols. 1–7, and before the Civil War included Arkansas, 1836, 1:269; California, 1849, 1:392; Connecticut, 1818, 1:537; Delaware, 1792, 5:465; Florida, 1838, 2:665; Illinois, 1818, 2:983, Indiana, 1816, 2:1037; Iowa, 1846, 2:1121; Kentucky, 1792, 3:1274; Maine, 1819, 3:1647, Michigan, 1835, 4:1831; Mississippi, 1817, 4:2033; Missouri, 1820, 4:2164; New Jersey, 1844, 4:2599; Ohio, 1802, 4:2910; Pennsylvania, 1790, 5:3100; Tennessee, 1792, 6:3423; Texas, 1836, 6:3542 and 3548; and Wisconsin, 1848, 7:4077. Other states follow common law or statutes.

17. Cooper, *Treatise*, p. 78.

18. United States v. Hudson and Goodwin, 7 Cranch 32 at 34 (U.S. 1812).

19. Ibid., p. 33.

20. Lawhorne, *Defamation*, pp. 70–85. Research yields only three criminal libel cases reaching appellate courts between the War of 1812 and the Civil War.

21. This doctrine started with People v. Croswell, 3 Johns. Cas. 337 (N.Y.

1804). Constitutional adoptions of the defense, in note 16, above, were made in Florida, Iowa, Michigan, New Jersey, and Wisconsin before the Civil War.

22. U.S., *Constitution,* Amend. 5; 1 *Stat.* 21.
23. Barron v. Mayor of Baltimore, 32 U.S. (7 Pet.) 243 at 246 (1833).
24. U.S., *Constitution,* art. III.
25. White v. Nichols, 3 How. 266 at 285 (U.S. 1845).
26. Ibid., p. 291.
27. Ibid., p. 292.
28. Ibid., p. 291.
29. Ibid., pp. 286–89.
30. Ibid., p. 290.
31. Lawhorne, *Defamation,* pp. 87–110 passim. Research shows that between the Civil War and the turn of the twentieth century some type of privilege was recognized in twenty-five of the twenty-eight jurisdictions in which appellate court decisions in public-official libel suits were recorded.
32. Some examples include Palmer v. Concord, 97 Am. Dec. 605 (N.H. 1865); Marks v. Baker, 9 N.W. 678 (Minn. 1881); State v. Balch, 2 Pac. 609 (Kan. 1884); Cotulla v. Kerr, 11 S.W. 1058 (Tex. 1889); Jackson v. Pittsburgh Times, 25 Atl. 513 (Pa. 1893); Augusta Evening News v. Radford, 17 S.E. 612 (Ga. 1893); Boucher v. Clark Pub. Co., 84 N.W. 237 (S.D. 1900); O'Rourke v. Leiston Daily Sun Pub. Co., 36 Atl. 398 (Me. 1900); Hamilton v. Eno, 81 N.Y. 116 (N.Y. 1800).
33. Some examples include Sweeney v. Baker, 31 Am. Rep. 757 (W. Va. 1878); Rearick v. Wilcox, 81 Ill. 77 (1876); Fitzpatrick v. Daily States Publ. Co., 20 So. 173 (La. 1896); Upton v. Hume, 33 Pac. 810 (Ore. 1893); Bronson v. Bruce, 26 N.W. 671 (Mich. 1886). The leading case for fair comment and criticism in this period was Burt v. Advertiser Newspaper Co., 28 N.E. 1 (Mass. 1891).
34. William G. Hale, *The Law of the Press* (Saint Paul: West Publishing Co., 1948), pp. 74–77. See Castle v. Houston, 19 Kan. 417 (1877) for a review of common-law holdings.
35. Wertz v. Sprecher, 118 N.W. 1071 (Neb. 1908) reviews the law here, listing Florida, Maine, and Massachusetts among such states. Hale, *The Law,* also lists Illinois, New Hampshire, and Wyoming as holding this view in early cases.
36. Dorr v. United States, 195 U.S. 138 at 148 (1904).
37. Ibid., p. 151.
38. Ibid., pp. 152–53.
39. Patterson v. Colorado, 250 U.S. 454 at 459–60 (1907).
40. U.S., *Constitution,* Amend. 14, sec. 1 (1868).

41. An excellent account of this case can be found in Irving Brant, *The Bill of Rights: Its Origin and Meaning* (New York: New American Library, 1965), pp. 387–91.
42. Patterson v. Colorado, 205 U.S. 452 at 461.
43. Ibid., p. 462.
44. Peck v. Tribune, 214 U.S. 185 at 189 (1909).
45. Ibid.
46. Ibid., p. 190.
47. Gandia v. Pettingill, 222 U.S. 452 at 458–59 (1912).
48. Ibid., p. 457.
49. This decision is an interesting contrast to that which Justice Holmes rendered in *Burt* v. *Advertiser Publishing Co.* when on the Massachusetts bench. In Burt v. Advertiser, 28 N.E. 1 at 4 (1891), Justice Holmes ruled that "what is privileged, if that is the proper term, is criticism, not statement." He also said that the interest is in freedom of discussion "rather than of statement." However, here, in *Gandia* v. *Pettingill,* Justice Holmes uses the identical words, "statement" and "comment," and states both are privileged in absence of express malice. The time span between the two cases was twenty years.
50. Nalle v. Oyster, 240 U.S. 165 at 182 (1913).
51. Baker v. Warner, 231 U.S. 588 at 594 (1913).
52. Washington Post Co. v. Chaloner, 250 U.S. 290 at 293 (1919). The only other defamation case the Supreme Court considered prior to World War I was Pollard v. Lyon, 91 U.S. 225 (1876), and it was a slander case with no real application to the libel actions under study.
53. Lawhorne, *Defamation,* pp. 111–75 passim. States limiting privilege to fair comment and criticism before World War I included Alabama, Arkansas, Illinois, Kentucky, Louisiana, Maine, Maryland, Massachusetts, Mississippi, New Jersey, New York, Ohio, Tennessee, Washington, and Wisconsin.
54. John D. Stevens, Robert L. Bailey, Judith F. Krueger, and John M. Mollwitz, "Criminal Libel as Seditious Libel, 1916, 1965," *Journalism Quarterly* 43, no. 1 (Spring 1966): 112. The count here is 235 criminal libel prosecutions in the last half of the nineteenth century compared to still fewer, 148, in the fifty years ending in 1965.
55. Prudential Insurance Co. v. Cheek, 259 U.S. 530 at 542–43 (1920). This case contested a Missouri law requiring employers to give employees leaving them for any reason a letter showing the true causes for leaving. The insurance company claimed its right of privacy was being violated by the state, in violation of the Fourteenth Amendment.

2. Revised View of the Constitution
State Press Decisions Can Be Nullified

1. Calvin D. Linton, ed., *The Bicentennial Almanac* (New York: Thomas Nelson, Inc., 1975), pp. 290–93. Nearly one thousand people were convicted under the Espionage Act of 1917 and the amendment of 1918. See 40 *Stat.* 217 at 219 and 40 *Stat.* 553.
2. U.S., *Constitution,* Amends. 17 19,
3. Education and communications also had undergone an explosive expansion, and radio allowed individuals to learn more quickly of developments in the world. The automobile and airplane "reduced" distances to different parts of the nation. Newspapers served by national wire services grew from one hundred to fourteen hundred between 1914 and 1940. See Frank Luther Mott, *American Journalism: A History* (New York: Macmillan Co., 1962), pp. 691–92, 710.
4. Gitlow v. New York, 268 U.S. 652 at 666 (1925).
5. Near v. Minnesota ex rel. Olson, 283 U.S. 697 at 707 (1931).
6. *Mason's Minnesota Statutes,* 1927, vol. 2, secs. 10123-1 to 10123-3, p. 1992.
7. Lamar T. Beman, *Selected Articles on Censorship of Speech and the Press* (New York: AMS Press, 1969), p. 243.
8. Near v. Minnesota ex rel. Olson, 283 U.S. at 713.
9. Ibid., p. 723.
10. Ibid., p. 721.
11. Ibid., p. 716.
12. Ibid., pp. 716–17.
13. Ibid., p. 723.
14. Ibid., pp. 718, 720.
15. Ibid., p. 715.
16. Ibid.
17. James J. Bierbower, "Fair Comment on a Political Candidate," *Georgetown Law Journal* 37, no. 3 (March 1949): 413. Also see Dix W. Noel, "Defamation of Public Officers and Candidates," *Columbia Law Review* 49, no. 7 (November 1949): 882.
18. Sweeney v. Philadelphia Record Co., 126 F.2d 53 (1942), held not libelous under Pennsylvania law of libel and privilege; Sweeny v. Patterson, 128 F.2d 457 at 458 (1942), discounted errors in fact and partially adopted liberal rule for the District of Columbia; Sweeney v. Caller-Times Pub. Co., 41 F. Supp. 163 at 168 (1941), held statements not libelous under Texas law granting privilege except when falsehoods are grounds for removal from office. In Schenectady Union Publishing Co. v.

Sweeney, 122 F.2d 288 (C.C.A.N.Y. 1941), the disposition of other cases is listed, p. 28, and it states Sweeney won his case in two unreported Illinois decisions.

19. Federal courts had to follow state law as well as state common law after the United States Supreme Court ruling in Erie Railroad Co. v. Thompkins, 403 U.S. 64 (1938).

20. Schenectady Union Pub. Co. v. Sweeney, 122 F.2d 288; dissent pp. 291–92.

21. Id., 316 U.S. 642 (1942).

22. See opinion in New York Times v. Sullivan, 376 U.S. 254 at 268 (1964), where the Court states that the *Schenectady Union* case was the only previous case considered by the Court in which constitutional limitations were a direct issue.

23. Lawhorne, *Defamation,* pp. 152–65, 173; states allowing privilege for nonmalicious falsehoods about officials include Arizona, California, Colorado, Connecticut, Iowa, Kansas, Michigan, Minnesota, Montana, Nebraska, New Hampshire, North Carolina, Pennsylvania, South Dakota, Utah, and West Virginia. It was partially subscribed to by Delaware, the District of Columbia, Oklahoma, Texas, and Wyoming. Half adopted this rule after World War I.

24. Lawhorne, *Defamation,* pp. 129–42, states limiting privilege to fair comment and criticism were Alabama, Arkansas, Florida, Hawaii, Illinois, Kentucky, Louisiana, Maine, Maryland, Massachusetts, Mississippi, New Jersey, New York, North Dakota, Ohio, Oregon, South Carolina, Tennessee, Vermont, Virginia, Washington, and Wisconsin. Fifteen of these states had adopted this narrow rule of privilege before World War I.

25. Beauharnais v. Illinois, 343 U.S. 250 at 253–54 (1951).

26. Ibid., p. 251.

27. Ibid., pp. 256–65, 266.

28. Ibid., p. 258.

29. Ibid., p. 264.

30. Ibid., p. 264–65.

31. Ibid., pp. 270–73.

32. Ibid., 256 n.5.

33. Ibid.

34. Donald M. Gillmor and Jerome A. Barron, *Mass Communication Law* (Saint Paul: West Publishing Co., 1974), p. 201.

35. Farmers Educational and Cooperative Union of America, North Dakota Division v. WDAY, Inc., 360 U.S. 525 at 531–35 (1959).

36. Federal Communications Act, 48 *Stat.* 1088 as amended by 47 *U.S.C.* sec. 315a.

37. Farmers Cooperative v. WDAY, Inc., 360 U.S. at 529–30.
38. See Associated Press v. United States, 326 U.S. 1 at 20 (1945), in which the Court states that First Amendment freedom rests "on the assumption that the widest possible dissemination of information from diverse and antagonistic sources is essential to the welfare of the public."
39. Barr v. Matteo, 360 U.S. 564 at 571, 575 (1959).
40. Ibid., p. 571.
41. Howard v. Lyons, 360 U.S. 514 at 797 (1959).
42. See comment in Garrison v. Louisiana, 379 U.S. 64 at 70 (1964), where the Proposed Official Draft of the Model Penal Code of the American Law Institute is quoted to the effect that penal control of personal defamation is inappropriate and "this probably accounts for the paucity of prosecutions and the near desuetude of private criminal libel legislation in this country."
43. Georgia, Idaho, Nevada, and Virginia joined the states listed in note 23 above; Colorado adopted an independent view. Lawhorne, *Defamation*, pp. 200–201, 209, 322 n.107.
44. The list in note 24 above was diminished only by Virginia. Other states had established no precedent or followed independent views. Lawhorne, *Defamation*, pp. 201, 322 n.108.

3. A New Constitutional Privilege
Libel Restricted by *New York Times* v. *Sullivan*

1. New York Times v. Sullivan, 376 U.S. 254 at 279–80 (1964). This case also included the decision to *Abernathy* v. *Sullivan*, which had been combined with the *New York Times* case by the Supreme Court.
2. Ibid., p. 264.
3. Ibid., p. 266.
4. Ibid., p. 257.
5. Ibid., pp. 257–58.
6. Ibid., pp. 258–59.
7. "The New Constitutional Definition of Libel and Its Future," *Northwestern University Law Review* 66, no. 1 (March–April 1965): 110. This study lists the largest libel judgment prior to this time at $67,000; it was reduced to $45,000.
8. See Shelly v. Kraemer, 334 U.S. 1 at 4 (1948), where the opinion reads "That the action of state courts and judicial officers in their official capacities is to be regarded as action of the State within the meaning of the Fourteenth Amendment, is a proposition which has long been established by decisions of this court."
9. New York Times v. Sullivan, 376 U.S. at 265.

10. See Valentine v. Chrestensen, 316 U.S. 52 at 54 (1942).
11. New York Times v. Sullivan, 376 U.S. at 266.
12. Ibid., p. 273.
13. Ibid., p. 268.
14. Ibid.
15. Ibid., p. 269.
16. Ibid., p. 273.
17. Ibid., p. 271.
18. Ibid., p. 273.
19. Ibid., p. 276.
20. Ibid., p. 279.
21. Ibid., p. 264.
22. L. Brent Bozall, *The Warren Revolution* (New Rochelle, N.Y.: Arlington House, 1966), pp. 34–35, stated the Supreme Court had instituted a new system of Constitution making. By reviewing state judgments, the Supreme Court became lawmakers, not expounders. This was the situation here.
23. New York Times v. Sullivan, 376 U.S. at 283.
24. Ibid., pp. 279–80.
25. Ibid., pp. 201–2. Justice Goldberg's concurring opinion, stresses that private defamation is not protected by the Constitution.
26. Ibid., pp. 294, 298.
27. Ibid., pp. 295, 304.
28. Ibid., p. 285. Also see Samuel Gray McNamara, "Recent Developments Concerning Constitutional Limitations on State Defamation Laws," *Vanderbilt Law Review* 18 (June 1965):1455.
29. New York Times v. Sullivan, 376 U.S. at 285 n.26.
30. Ibid., p. 286.
31. Ibid., p. 287.
32. Ibid., p. 286.
33. Ibid., p. 287.
34. Ibid.
35. Ibid.
36. Ibid., p. 286.
37. Ibid., p. 288.
38. Ibid., p. 293.
39. Ibid.
40. Discussions of this can be found in Harold J. Spaeth, *The Warren Court* (San Francisco: Chandler Publishing Co., 1966), p. 151; McNamara, "State Defamation Laws," p. 1453; and "Libel and Its Future," p. 102.
41. The *New York Times* decision also settled the *Abernathy* case.

42. The Court said the *Times* gave up any possible conflict as far as diversity of citizenship claims by putting in an appearance in state court. New York Times v. Sullivan, 376 U.S. at 264 n.4.
43. Spaeth, *The Warren Court*, p. 151.
44. New York Times v. Sullivan, 376 U.S. at 294–95.
45. Ibid., p. 270.
46. Ibid., p. 283.

4. An Expanded "Public-Official Rule" Limits Public Employee, Union, Criminal Libels

1. Garrison v. Louisiana, 379 U.S. 64 at 77 (1964).
2. Rosenblatt v. Baer, 383 U.S. 75 at 85 (1966).
3. Linn v. United Plant Guard Workers of America Local 114, 383 U.S. 53 (1966).
4. Garrison v. Louisiana, 379 U.S. at 66.
5. Ibid., p. 77.
6. Ibid., p. 73.
7. Ibid., pp. 70–71 n.7.
8. Ibid., p. 74.
9. Ibid., p. 75.
10. Ibid., p. 79.
11. Ibid.
12. See Barr v. Matteo, 360 U.S. 564 (1959), discussed in chap. 2.
13. New York Times v. Sullivan, 376 U.S. at 282–83; Garrison v. Louisiana, 379 U.S. at 74.
14. Henry v. Collins joined with Henry v. Persons, 380 U.S. 356 at 357 (1965).
15. Garrison v. Louisiana, 379 U.S. at 69.
16. Ibid., p. 70.
17. Ibid.
18. Ashton v. Kentucky, 384 U.S. 195 at 198 (1965).
19. Ibid.
20. Ibid., p. 200.
21. See NLRB v. Drivers Local 639, 362 U.S. 274 at 279 (1960), quoting the National Labor Relations Act, 29 U.S.C. sec. 157.
22. Linn v. United Plant Guard Workers of American Local 114, 383 U.S. 53 (1966). This was a 6–3 decision. See 15 L. Ed. 2d. 582 at 586, 589, and 591 for actual malice and actual injury rulings.
23. Rosenblatt v. Baer, 383 U.S. 75 at 85 (1966).
24. Ibid., pp. 79, 82.
25. Ibid., p. 82.

26. Ibid., p. 81.
27. Ibid., p. 82.
28. Ibid., p. 84.
29. Ibid., p. 85.
30. Ibid., p. 87 n.13. Also see p. 86 of decision.
31. Ibid., p. 88.
32. Ibid., p. 88 n.15.
33. Ibid., p. 87.
34. The New Hampshire Supreme Court after this ruled that Baer on retrial was entitled to have a jury determination about whether he was a public official and whether a privileged occasion existed. See Baer v. Rosenblatt, 237 A.2d 130 (N.H. 1967).
35. Rosenblatt v. Baer, 383 U.S. at 84.
36. Ibid., p. 100.
37. Ibid., p. 94.
38. Ibid., p. 100.
39. Ibid., p. 93.
40. Ibid., p. 86.
41. Ibid., p. 85.
42. See Commonwealth v. Armano, 285 A.2d 626 (1972) for Pennsylvania; Weston v. State, 528 S.W.2d 412 (1975) for Arkansas; Eberle v. Municipal Court, 127 Cal. Rptn. 594 (1976) for California.
43. Marc A. Franklin, "Teacher's Manual," *The First Amendment and the Fourth Estate* (Mineola, N.Y.: Foundation Press, 1977), p. 61.
44. Lawhorne, *Defamation*, p. 260, citing Matassa v. Bel, 164 So. 2d 332 (La. 1964); and Tucker v. Kilgore, 338 S.W.2d 112 (Ky. 1964).
45. Lawhorne, *Defamation*, pp. 233–64.
46. Turley v. WTAX, Inc., 236 N.E.2d 778 (Ill. 1966), architect on a public building; Arizona Biochemical Co. v. Hearst Co., 280 F. Supp. 412 (1969), garbage collection agency; Doctors Convalescent Center, Inc., v. East Shore Newspapers, Inc., 244 N.E.2d 373 (Ill. 1968), operators of nursing home.
47. Klahr v. Winterble, 418 P.2d 404 (Ariz. 1966).
48. See Short v. News-Journal Co., 212 A.2d 716 (Del. 1954); Sheridan v. Crisona, 198 N.E.2d 359 (N.Y., 1964); Williams v. Daily Review, Inc., 46 Cal. Rptr. 135 (1965); Lulay v. Peoria Journal-Star, Inc., 214 N.E.2d 746 (Ill. 1966).
49. See Pauling v. News Syndicate Co., 335 F.2d 659 (1964); Pauling v. Globe Democrat, 362 F.2d 188 (1966); Pauling v. National Review, 269 N.Y.S.2d 11 (1966); Gilbert v. Goffi, 251 N.Y.S.2d 823 (1964); Pearson v. Fairbanks Publishing Co., 413 P.2d 711 (Alaska 1966); Clark v. Allen, 204 A.2d 42 (Pa. 1964).

5. Privilege to Discuss Public Figures
Libels Bound by Public-Official Rule

1. See notes 45–48, chap. 4.
2. Rosenblatt v. Baer, 383 U.S. 75 at 85 (1966).
3. Curtis Publishing Co. v. Butts, 388 U.S. 130 at 164, 170, 172 (1967). This case includes *Associated Press* v. *Walker.* The separate page citations include separate endorsements of the actual malice standard by Warren, Black, Douglas, Brennan, and White.
4. Time, Inc., v. Hill, 385 U.S. 374 at 388 (1967).
5. Ibid., p. 378.
6. Ibid., p. 377.
7. Ibid., p. 388.
8. Ibid.
9. Ibid., pp. 388–89.
10. William E. Francois, *Mass Media Law and Regulation,* 2d ed. (Columbus, Ohio: Grid, Inc., 1978), p. 172.
11. Time, Inc., v. Hill, 385 U.S. 374 at 390.
12. Ibid., p. 391.
13. Ibid.
14. Curtis Publishing Co. v. Butts, 388 U.S. 130 at 136 (1967).
15. Ibid.
16. Ibid.
17. Ibid., p. 137.
18. Ibid., pp. 161 n.23, 169.
19. Ibid., p. 137.
20. Butts v. Curtis Publishing Co. 242 F. Supp. 390 (1964).
21. Curtis Publishing Co. v. Butts, 388 U.S. at 159 n.22.
22. *New York Times,* 12 June 1967, p. 1, cols. 2–3. Also see Walker v. Louisville Courier-Journal and Louisville Times Co., 246 F. Supp. 231 (1965); and Walker v. Associated Press, 191 So. 2d 727 (La. 1966). In Walker v. Pulitzer Publishing Co., 394 F.2d 800 (1969), a list of the suits is included on p. 807. Walker sued the Associated Press in Arkansas, Florida, and Texas. He also brought suits against the *Saint Louis Post Dispatch,* the *New Orleans Times-Picayune,* the *Denver Post,* the *Kansas City Star,* the *Louisville Courier-Journal,* the *Atlanta Journal,* the *Arkansas Gazette,* and the *Arkansas Democrat* for printing the same article. He lost them all, with the exception of a reduced judgment in a Louisiana suit against the Associated Press.
23. Curtis Publishing Co. v. Butts, 388 U.S. at 142.
24. Ibid., p. 134.
25. Ibid., pp. 134–35, where some twenty cases are cited in n.1.

26. Ibid., p. 135.
27. Ibid., pp. 146–47.
28. Ibid., p. 147, quoting "Letter to the Inhabitants of Quebec," *Journal of Continental Congress*, p. 108.
29. Ibid., pp. 148, 162.
30. Ibid., p. 155.
31. Ibid., pp. 155, 162, 164.
32. Ibid., pp. 153, 163–64.
33. Ibid., p. 155.
34. Ibid., p. 163.
35. Ibid., Black and Douglas, p. 170; Brennan and White, p. 172.
36. Ibid., pp. 164–65.
37. Ibid., pp. 163–64.
38. Ibid., p. 164.
39. Ibid., pp. 165, 170, 172.
40. Ibid., p. 159.
41. Ibid., p. 158.
42. Ibid., p. 170.
43. Ibid.
44. Ibid.
45. Ibid., p. 161 n.23.
46. Ibid., p. 172.
47. Ibid., p. 174.
48. Ibid., pp. 170–71.
49. Ibid., p. 171.
50. Ibid., pp. 159–69.
51. There of course could be procedural due process reviews by the Court to determine if fair trials had been given. See "The New Constitutional Definition of Libel and Its Future," *Northwestern University Law Review* 66, no. 1 (March–April 1965): 104–6. There also is precedent for the Supreme Court's backing out of substantive due process reviews when governmental regulation was bound by reasonableness. See Nebbia v. New York, 291 U.S. 502 (1934).
52. Within four months after the public-figure ruling, lower courts implemented the standard. Rose v. Koch, 154 N.W.2d 409 (Minn. 1967); Grayson v. Curtis Publishing Co., 436 P.2d 756 (Wash. 1968); El Paso Times, Inc., v. Trexler, 447 S.W.2d 403 (Tex. 1969); Tilton v. Cowles Pub. Co., 459 P.2d 8 (Calif. 1959); Carrito v. Time, Inc., 302 F. Supp. 107 (Calif. 1959); Trait v. King Broadcasting Co., 460 P.2d 307 (Wash. 1969); Time, Inc., v. McLaney, 407 F.2d 565 (Fla. 1969); Aber v. Stahlin, 159 N.W.2d 156 (Mich. 1968) are cases that are representative of those determined in lower courts.

6. A Constitutional Command
Libel Rule Is Explained, Enforced

1. See Harmon Zeigler, *Interest Groups in American Society* (Englewood Cliffs, N.J.: Prentice-Hall, Inc., 1965), pp. 328–29, where he discussed possible ways to erode Supreme Court decisions—by legal questions, hostile interpretation, and noncompliance.
2. Beckley Newspapers Corp. v. Hanks, 389 U.S. 81, 19 L. Ed. 2d 248 at 250. The Supreme Court of Appeals for West Virginia denied review.
3. Id., 19 L. Ed. 2d 248 at 252.
4. Ibid., p. 250.
5. Ibid., p. 252.
6. Ibid., p. 251.
7. St. Amant v. Thompson, 390 U.S. 727 at 730.
8. Ibid., p. 732.
9. Thompson v. St. Amant, 184 So. 314 at 321–23 (La. 1966).
10. Id., 196 So. 2d 255 at 262 (La. 1967).
11. St. Amant v. Thompson, 390 U.S. 727, Justice Abe Fortas dissented, stating that if a public official is "needlessly, heedlessly, falsely accused of crime," he should have a remedy in law, p. 734.
12. Ibid., p. 731.
13. Ibid.
14. Ibid.
15. Ibid., quote of Curtis Publishing Co. v. Butts, 388 U.S. 130 at 153.
16. St. Amant v. Thompson, 390 U.S. 727 at 731.
17. Ibid., p. 732.
18. Tunnell v. the Edwardsville Intelligencer, Inc., 252 N.E.2d 28 (Ill. 1969), 38 L.W. 3388 (4-7-70), an editorial writer's statement that the city attorney was going to break the law by not enforcing it; Tagawa v. Maui Publishing Co., Ltd., 38 L.W. 3122 (1969), a story in a Hawaii newspaper saying county official had used county equipment on his property. Reporter had seen use but had not checked to see if official had paid for use. Newspapers were upheld in both instances. Also see Goldwater v. Ginzburg, 396 U.S. 1049.
19. *Editor and Publisher*, 1 June 1968, p. 60, col. 3; *New York Times*, 25 May 1968, p. 1, col. 2.
20. Goldwater v. Ginzburg, 261 F. Supp. 784 at 787 (1966).
21. Ginzburg never did dispute that the article was false but did say it was fair opinion and that it was vital to free debate to discuss fitness for the presidency. He testified that he was not interested in truth or falsity, that

he wanted to show what psychiatrists said. *New York Times,* 25 May 1969, p. 22.

22. Ginzburg v. Goldwater, 396 U.S. 1049, 38 L.W. 3280 (1-27-70).
23. Id., 38 L.W. 3288.
24. Greenbelt Cooperative Publishing Assoc. v. Bresler, 398 U.S. 6 at 9 (1970).
25. Ibid., p. 10-11.
26. Ibid., p. 13.
27. Ibid.
28. Ibid., p. 12.
29. Monitor Patriot Co. v. Roy, 401 U.S. 265 (1971).
30. Ibid., p. 269.
31. Ibid., p. 272.
32. Ibid., p. 271.
33. Ibid., p. 275.
34. Ibid., p. 274.
35. Ibid.
36. Ibid., p. 276.
37. Ibid., p. 277.
38. Ibid.
39. Ibid., p. 276.
40. Ocala Star-Banner Co. v. Damron, 401 U.S. 295.
41. Ibid., p. 298.
42. Ibid., p. 301.
43. Time, Inc., v. Pape, 401 U.S. 279 (1971).
44. Ibid., p. 287.
45. Ibid., pp. 287–89.
46. Ibid., pp. 289–90.
47. Pape v. Time, Inc., 354 F.2d 558 at 559 (7th Cir. 1965).
48. Time, Inc., v. Pape, 401 U.S. 279 at 289.
49. Ibid., p. 290.
50. Ibid., p. 291.
51. Ibid., p. 292.
52. Ibid.
53. Ibid.
54. Ibid., p. 285.

7. A Constitutional Dilemma
Court Splits on Privilege to Discuss Issues

1. Rosenbloom v. Metromedia, Inc., 403 U.S. 29 at 52 (1971).
2. Ibid., p. 59.

3. Ibid., pp. 34–35.
4. Ibid., p. 36.
5. Ibid., pp. 39–40.
6. Ibid., p. 44.
7. Ibid.
8. Ibid., p. 41.
9. Ibid., p. 43.
10. Ibid., p. 45.
11. Ibid., p. 50.
12. Ibid., p. 48.
13. Ibid.
14. Ibid., pp. 50–51.
15. Ibid., p. 56.
16. Ibid., p. 57.
17. Ibid., p. 59.
18. Ibid., p. 61.
19. Ibid., p. 62.
20. Ibid.
21. Ibid., p. 60.
22. Ibid., pp. 62, 81.
23. Ibid., pp. 63, 81.
24. Ibid.
25. Ibid., p. 63.
26. Ibid., pp. 70, 86.
27. Ibid., p. 84.
28. Ibid., p. 86.
29. Ibid., pp. 74–77 passim.
30. Ibid., p. 77.
31. Ibid., p. 75.
32. Ibid., pp. 78, 87.
33. Ibid., pp. 70, 72, 83, 86.
34. Ibid.
35. Ibid., pp. 77, 86.
36. Ibid., pp. 69–70.
37. Ibid., pp. 70–71.
38. Ibid., p. 58.
39. Firestone v. Time, Inc., 400 F.2d 721 (1972), electronic evesdropping; Thuma v. Hearst Corp. 840 F. Supp. 423 (D.C. Md. 1972), shooting of boy by police; Anderson v. Guard Pub. Co., 489 P.2d 946 (Ore. 1971), shooting in divorce case; Nigro v. Miami Herald Publishing Co., 262 So. 2d 698 (3d Cir. 1972), organized crime; Cerrito v. Time, Inc., 449 F.2d 306 (9th Cir. 1971), organized crime; Time, Inc., v. Johnston, 448 F.2d

378 (1971), sports figures; Goldman v. Time, Inc., 336 F. Supp. 133 (1971), backpacking in Crete; O'Brien v. Tribune Pub. Co., 499 P.2d 27 (Wash. 1972), pollution worker; Polzen v. Helmbrech, 196 N.W.3d 689 (Wisc. 1972), pollution dispute; Steak Bit of Westbury, Inc., v. Newsday, 334 N.Y.S.2d 330 (1971), eating places of public concern; Autobusses Internationales v. Centenial Pub. Co., 438 S.W.2d 508 (Tex. 1972), private bus company of public interest; Bannach v. Field Enterprises, 284 N.E.2d 31 (Ill. 1972), suspended student of public concern; West v. Northern Pub. Co., 487 P.2d 1304 (Alaska 1971), selling liquor to minors of concern to public; Firestone v. Time, Inc., 271 So. 2d 745 (Fla. 1972), divorce matter of public concern; Treutler v. Meredith, 455 F.2d 259 (8th Cir. 1972), books of public interest; Gordon v. Random House, 349 F. Supp. 919 (D.C. Pa. 1972), book on riots of public interest; Harnish v. Herald Mail Co., 286 A.2d 151 (Md. 1972), housing eviction of public interest; McFarland v. Hearst Corp., 332 F. Supp. 746 (1971), escape from jail of public interest; Miller v. Argus Publishing Co., 490 P.2d 101 (Wash. 1971), role in political campaign of public interest; Credit Bureau of Dalton, Inc., v. CBS News, 332 F. Supp. 1291 (1971), practices of credit bureau of public interest; Schwartz v. Time, Inc., 337 N.Y.2d 125 (1972), organized crime of public interest.

40. See Obeman v. Dunn and Bradstreet, 460 F.2d 1383 (7th Cir. 1972); and Hood v. Dunn and Bradstreet, 335 F. Supp. 170 (1971), both of which held public interest not extended to credit company reports concerning individual credit.

41. See John L. Geldmacher and James A. Lumpp, "Rosenbloom and Libel," *Freedom of Information Center Report*, no. 297, p. 5, citing six law review articles taking this view.

42. See Gertz v. Welch, 418 U.S. 323, 94 S. Ct. 2997, 41 L. Ed. 2d 789 at 827, where Justice White lists seventeen states and six courts of appeals at the federal level adopting the *Rosenbloom* plurality decision before June 1974.

8. Privilege to Discuss Individuals
"Private Libel" Confined by *Gertz* v. *Welch*

1. See Justice Byron White's opinion, Gertz v. Welch, 41 L. Ed. 2d 789 at 827 (1974). A listing of all the jurisdictions adopting the *Rosenbloom* plurality view is on pp. 827–28 n.10.

2. Gertz v. Welch, 418 U.S. 323, 94 S. Ct. 2997, 41 L. Ed. 2d 789 at 797 (1974).

3. Id., 41 L. Ed. 2d at 813, Justice Blackmun's opinion.

4. Ibid., p. 833, words of Justice White; also p. 809.

5. Ibid., p. 811.
6. Ibid., p. 828, statement of Justice White.
7. Ibid., pp. 807, 813, 814, 817, 822, and 838.
8. Ibid., p. 806.
9. Ibid., p. 813, where Justice Blackmun equates fault and negligence.
10. Gertz v. Welch, 322 F. Supp. 997 (N.D. Ill. 1970).
11. Id., 41 L. Ed. 2d 789 at 812.
12. Id., 471 F.2d 801 at 809 (7th Cir. 1971).
13. Id., 41 L. Ed. 2d at 801.
14. Ibid.
15. Ibid., p. 807.
16. Ibid., n. 8.
17. Ibid., p. 807.
18. Ibid., p. 806.
19. Ibid., p. 807.
20. Ibid.
21. Ibid., p. 808.
22. Ibid., p. 809.
23. Ibid., pp. 809–10.
24. See White's opinion, Ibid., p. 833 n.27.
25. Ibid., p. 811.
26. Ibid., p. 808.
27. Curtis Publishing Co. v. Butts, 388 U.S. 130 at 163–64, opinion of Chief Justice Earl Warren.
28. Gertz v. Welch, 41 L. Ed. 2d at 812.
29. Ibid.
30. Ibid.
31. Ibid.
32. Ibid., p. 813. At the time this book was written, the retrial was pending, with the only remaining issues being "fault" and "damages." Gertz had obtained a summary judgment on retrial, to the effect that he was a private person and that defamatory falsehoods were involved. See William E. Francois, *1978 Yearbook: Mass Media Law and Regulation* (Columbus, Ohio: Grid, Inc., 1978), p. 8.
33. Gertz v. Welch, 41 L. Ed. 2d at 813.
34. Ibid., p. 814.
35. Ibid., pp. 823, 838, 840.
36. Ibid., p. 833.
37. Ibid., p. 821.
38. Ibid., p. 817.
39. Ibid., p. 814.
40. Ibid., p. 802.

41. Old Dominion Branch No. 496, National Association of Letter Carriers, AFL-CIO v. Austin, 418 U.S. 264 (1974).
42. Ibid., p. 279. See p. 285 for "rhetorical hyperbole" statement.
43. Ibid., p. 291.
44. The Court's opinion used terms such as media, broadcaster, and publisher, and some commentary speculated as to the holding being limited to media defendants only. Legal definitions are not so confining. See Henry Campbell Black, *Black's Law Dictionary,* 5th ed. (St. Paul: West Publishing Co., 1979), pp. 1105, 1109. Publication, in legal terms, means "communicating of libelous matter to a third person." The definition of publisher includes one who, by himself and without an agent, makes something publicly known. This is the view taken by court decisions. See Davis v. Schuchat, 510 F.2d 731 (D.C. Cir. 1975); Bryan v. Brown, 339 So. 2d 577 (Ala. 1976), *cert. denied,* 431 U.S. 954 (1977); Sewell v. Brookbank, 581 P.2d 267 (Ariz. App. 1978); Williams v. Trust Co. of Georgia, 230 S.E.2d 45 (Ga. App. 1976); Troman v. Wood, 340 N.E.2d 292 (Ill. 1975); Michaud v. Inhabitants of Town of Livermore Falls, 381 A.2d 1110 (Me. 1978); Martonik v. Durkan, 596 P.2d 1054 (Wash. App. 1979); Maheu v. Hughes Tool Co., 569 F.2d 459 (9th Cir. 1978). Dicta in some cases, however, have indicated the constitutional privilege is limited to publishers and broadcasters. See Foster v. Laredo Newspapers, Inc., 546 S.W.2d 809 (Tex. 1976); Martin v. Griffin Television, Inc., 549 P.2d 85 (Okla. 1976).
45. Aafco Hearing and Air Conditioning Co. v. Northwest Pub., Inc., 321 N.E.2d 580 (Ind. App. 1974), *cert. denied,* 424 U.S. 913; Walker v. Colorado Springs Sun, Inc., 538 P.2d 450 (Colo. 1974), *cert. denied,* 423 U.S. 1025 (1975).
46. See Chapadeau v. Utica Observer Dispatch 341 N.E.2d 569 (1975), where New York adopted the gross negligence test; Stone v. Essex County Newspapers, Inc., 330 N.E.2d 161 (1975), where Massachusetts denied punitive damages. Also see Peisner v. Detroit Free Press, 4 Med. L. Rept. 1062, 8 August 1978, where actual malice proof was required in reports of judicial proceedings, and Ryder v. Time, Inc., 3 Med. L. Rept. 1170, 1 November 1977, where a U.S. magistrate ruled that Virginia's standard was actual malice, though not as stringent at the *New York Times* rule.
47. Erick L. Collins and J. Doyle Drushal, "The Reaction of the State Courts to Gertz v. Robert Welch," *Case Western Reserve Law Review* 28 (Winter 1978): 306–25, particularly p. 313.
48. Ibid., pp. 311–12.
49. See note 27 above.
50. Discussion of various cases in Harry W. Stonecipher and Robert

Trager, "The Impact of Gertz on the Law of Libel," *Journalism Quarterly* 53 (Winter 1976): 609–18.

51. Statement made by Judge Alexander A. Lawrence in Rosanov v. Playboy Enterprises, Inc., 411 F. Supp. 440 at 443 (S.D. Ga. 1976).

9. A Constitutional Accommodation
Libel Recovery Clearly Is Not Foreclosed

1. Time, Inc., v. Firestone, 96 S. Ct. 958, 424 U.S. 440 at 451 (1976).
2. Id., 279 So. 2d 389.
3. Firestone v. Time, Inc., 305 So. 2d 172 at 178.
4. Time, Inc., v. Firestone, 424 U.S. 448 at 452.
5. Ibid., pp. 453–54.
6. Ibid., p. 457.
7. Ibid., p. 464. Mrs. Firestone, who married John Asher, dropped the action against Time, stating that she felt vindicated by the jury verdict earlier. This occurred in September 1978. See *Editor and Publisher*, 16 September 1978, p. 11.
8. Time, Inc., v. Firestone, 424 U.S. 448 at 464.
9. Ibid., p. 470.
10. Ibid., p. 485.
11. Ibid., p. 484.
12. Ibid., pp. 476–81 passim.
13. See Bruce W. Sanford, "Libel: A Year After Time v. Firestone," *Editor and Publisher*, 7 January 1978, p. 20, where he lists Johnny Carson and William Buckley, Jr., as pervasive public figures and John Dean and Elizabeth Ray as public figures for particular issues.
14. Herbert v. Lando, 3 Med. L. Rept. 1241 at 1247 (2d Cir. 1977).
15. Id., 60 L. Ed. 2d 115 at 124.
16. Ibid., pp. 129–30.
17. Ibid., p. 130.
18. New York Times v. Sullivan, 376 U.S. 254 at 287.
19. Herbert v. Lando, 60 L. Ed. 2d 115 at 127–28.
20. Ibid., pp. 135–36.
21. Ibid., p. 133.
22. Bruce W. Sanford, "No Quarter From This Court," *Columbia Journalism Review*, September–October 1979, pp. 59–63; "U.S. Journalists Alarmed at Court's New Libel Rule," *International Herald Tribune*, p. 1.
23. Sanford, "No Quarter," p. 60.
24. William J. Brennan, Jr., "Press and Court: Is the Strain Necessary?" *Editor and Publisher*, 27 October 1979, pp. 10, 33–34, specifically 33.

25. Sanford, "No Quarter," p. 60.
26. Wolston v. Reader's Digest 61 L. Ed. 2d 450 at 455–57 passim; also n.9.
27. Ibid., p. 495. Also see 578 F.2d 427.
28. Wolston v. Reader's Digest, 61 L. Ed. 2d at 458.
29. Ibid., p. 459.
30. Ibid., p. 460.
31. Ibid.
32. Ibid., p. 461.
33. Ibid.
34. *Webster's New World Dictionary of the American Language,* College Ed. (Cleveland: The World Publishing Co., 1962), p. 348.
35. Wolston v. Reader's Digest, 61 L. Ed. 2d at 461.
36. Sanford, "No Quarter," p. 62.
37. Wolston v. Reader's Digest, 61 L. Ed. 2d at 462.
38. Ibid.
39. Hutchinson v. Proxmire 61 L. Ed. 2d 411 at 419.
40. Ibid., p. 420.
41. Ibid., pp. 426–27.
42. Ibid., pp. 428 and 419 n.3, discussing *Congressional Record.*
43. Ibid., p. 430.
44. Ibid., pp. 431–32.
45. Ibid., p. 431.
46. Ibid., p. 421 n.8.
47. Rosenblatt v. Baer, 383 U.S. 75 at 85 (1966).
48. Beckley Newspapers Corp. v. Hanks, 389 U.S. 81. The Court here said there was not even an issue for the judge to send to the jury, which was tantamount to saying there should have been a summary judgment. Time, Inc., v. Pape, 401 U.S. 279 (1971), in which the summary judgment of the U.S. district court was upheld. Rosenblatt v. Baer, 383 U.S. 75 (1966).
49. Rosenblatt v. Baer, 383 U.S. at 88.
50. Hutchinson v. Proxmire, 61 L. Ed. 2d at 421 n.8.
51. Garrison v. Louisiana, 379 U.S. 64 (1964).
52. St. Amant v. Thompson, 390 U.S. 727 (1968).
53. "The Libel War Escalates," the *National Law Journal* 2, no. 32 (21 April 1980): 1, 26. The head of the libel department of the largest media insurer in the United States stated that libel claims had trippled in frequency over a two-year period. Some other insurance spokesmen laid the increase to the corresponding increase in the number of clients.
54. Ibid., p. 26. The figure listed in 1975 was 74; that of 1979 was listed at 112.

55. As an example, see American Broadcasting Co. v. Vegod Corp., 43 L.W. 3116–16 (1980), a case which the U.S. Supreme Court had been asked to review at the time this book was going to press. Here a television newscaster, quoting a Better Business Bureau claim, stated the corporation was deceiving the public while conducting a closeout sale for a "landmark" department store. The California courts, 603 P.2d 14, stated that the corporation was not a public figure as "criticism of commercial conduct does not merit special protection of actual malice."

56. A more restrictive view concerning summary judgments can be found in De Toledano v. Nader, 5 Med. L. Rptr. 1550 (D.C. Cir. 1980), *cert. denied*, 48 L.W. 3509. Here the court refused a summary judgment in a syndicated columnist's report, taken from a Senate subcommittee report, stating Ralph Nader distorted evidence. The court said there was an issue of actual malice. However a number of summary judgments have been granted. See Cefalu v. Globe Newspaper Co., 48 L.W. 3509 (1980), *cert. denied*, 48 L.W. 3534; Crosman v. Long Island University, 417 N.Y.S.2d 207, *cert. denied*, 48 L.W. 3733; Yiamouyiannis v. Consumers Union of the United States, Inc., 49 L.W. 3039 (1980); Raymer v. Doubleday & Co., 615 F.2d 241 (CA 5 1980); Southard v. Forbes Inc., 588 F.2d 140, *cert. denied*, 48 L.W. 3218 (1980).

TABLE
OF CASES

INDEX